BON

The L. Ron Hubbard Series
___

BRIDGE PUBLICATIONS, INC.
5600 E. Olympic Blvd.
Commerce, California 90022 USA

ISBN 978-1-4031-9886-0

© 1996, 2012 L. Ron Hubbard Library. All Rights Reserved.

Any unauthorized copying, translation, duplication, importation or distribution, in whole or in part, by any means, including electronic copying, storage or transmission, is a violation of applicable laws.

Special acknowledgment is made to the L. Ron Hubbard Library for permission to reproduce photographs from his personal collection. Additional credits: pp. cover, 114 Barratts Photo Press Ltd.; pp. 1, 7, 31, 51, 75, 99, 115, back cover caesart/Shutterstock.com; pp. 4–5 Stacey Lynn Payne/Shutterstock.com; pp. 8–9 Karl Weatherly/Getty Images; p. 13 American Stock Photography, Inc.; p. 18 George Marks/Getty Images; pp. 24–25 Archive Holdings Inc./Getty Images; pp. 48–49 Anton Foltin/Shutterstock.com; pp. 56–57 Marketa Mark/Shutterstock.com; pp. 82–83 Al Monner/Historic Photo Archive.net; p. 87 Pacific School of Religion; pp. 96–97 Anna Kucherova/Shutterstock.com; p. 107 M Reel/Shutterstock.com.

Dianetics, Scientology, Hubbard, OT, The Bridge, HCO, L. Ron Hubbard, LRH, Power, Power Plus, Saint Hill, LRH Device, Dianetics Symbol, Scientology Symbol, Scientology Cross (pointed), OT Symbol, Ron Signature and *L. Ron Hubbard Signature* are trademarks and service marks owned by Religious Technology Center and are used with its permission.

Scientologist is a collective membership mark designating members of the affiliated churches and missions of Scientology.

Bridge Publications, Inc. is a registered trademark and service mark in California and it is owned by Bridge Publications, Inc.

NEW ERA is a trademark and service mark owned by New Era Publications International ApS and is registered in Denmark, among other countries.

Printed in the United States of America

The L. Ron Hubbard Series: Philosopher & Founder—English

The L. Ron Hubbard Series

PHILOSOPHER & FOUNDER
REDISCOVERY OF THE HUMAN SOUL

Bridge
PUBLICATIONS, INC.®

CONTENTS

Philosopher & Founder: Rediscovery of the Human Soul

An Introduction to L. Ron Hubbard | 1

A Note on Survive and "Excalibur" | 7
　Excalibur *by L. Ron Hubbard* | 13
　Tomorrow's Miracles *by L. Ron Hubbard* | 19

The Birth of Dianetics | 31
　A Synopsis of Dianetics *by L. Ron Hubbard* | 35

The Golden Dawn of Scientology | 51
　Man's Search for His Soul *by L. Ron Hubbard* | 55
　Is It Possible to Be Happy? *by L. Ron Hubbard* | 59
　What Is Scientology? *by L. Ron Hubbard* | 65

A Word on Rediscovering the Human Soul | 75
　The Rediscovery of the Human Soul *by L. Ron Hubbard* | 79
　L. Ron Hubbard Discusses the Development of His Philosophy | 87

The Demystification of Death | 99
　A Note on Past Lives *by L. Ron Hubbard* | 105

The Bridge | 115
　The States of Existence *by L. Ron Hubbard* | 119
　Philosophy Wins after 2,000 Years *by L. Ron Hubbard* | 125
　Scientology Answers *by L. Ron Hubbard* | 129
　Dianetics, Scientology and Beyond *by L. Ron Hubbard* | 133
　My Only Defense for Having Lived *by L. Ron Hubbard* | 137
　My Philosophy *by L. Ron Hubbard* | 147

Epilogue | 155

Appendix
　Glossary | 159
　Index | 217

An Introduction to L. Ron Hubbard

The materials of Scientology comprise the largest written and spoken body of any single philosophic work. Those materials have further given rise to the only major religion founded in the twentieth century, and so stand as the spiritual cornerstone for several million adherents across all continents. It was additionally through the philosophy of Scientology that L. Ron Hubbard derived his solutions to criminality, drug addiction, illiteracy and social unrest—all now utilized by many millions more in virtually every nation on Earth. Yet when we examine the principles upon which that philosophy was founded, we find a truly simple conviction. In the first place, L. Ron Hubbard tells us, wisdom is meant for those who would reach for it and should never be regarded with awe. Next, he tells us that philosophic knowledge is only relevant to our lives if we can actually apply it, for "Learning locked in mildewed books is of little use to anyone." Finally, he tells us that philosophy has no value unless workable or true, and if we come to know the truth about ourselves, then the truth shall set us free.

Presented in the pages to follow are fifteen L. Ron Hubbard articles telling of his philosophic journey to the founding of Dianetics and Scientology. As word of introduction, let us first define *philosophy* as a love of wisdom or pursuit of wisdom and say that it traditionally embraces all grand quests for truth. Next, and specifically within that context, let us appreciate the work of L. Ron Hubbard as standing in the oldest philosophic tradition, extending back to at least the dawn of religious thought. Finally, let us describe Scientology as an *applied* religious philosophy and understand it rests not upon theory or assumption, but upon axioms derived from precise observation. Indeed, when we speak of Ron's philosophic journey, we are actually speaking of the first deliberate and methodical examination of spiritual matters wherein the only criteria had been one of workability. That is, did procedures derived from this quest actually

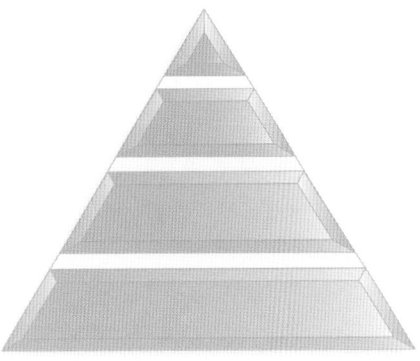

better our capability to survive, actually make us happier, more causative and more able? In that regard, then, we are not speaking of philosophy in any generally conceived sense: a discourse on existence, a contemplation of reality or a statement of our place in this world. Nor are we speaking of what passes for philosophy in the face of a materialist creed wherein all philosophic thought becomes meaningless beyond such grim platitudes as: *Your life is a biological accident, so you might as well get what you can before you die.* Rather, we are dealing with philosophy as derived from a search for *what is,* for truths that are workable, relevant and applicable to every facet of our lives. Or as Ron himself expressed it, "We are dealing with *discoveries.*"

At the heart of those discoveries lies a truly startling vision of Man as an intrinsically spiritual being who lives not eighty or so years before death makes us nothing, but, in fact, forever. How we might realize that vision is through the process of *auditing,* which is the central practice of Scientology and defined as the application of Scientology procedures by an auditor (from the Latin *audire,* to listen). Auditing is a highly precise activity and rests upon the principle that if we can truly grasp the source of what troubles us, then we are no

"We are studying the soul or spirit. We are studying it as itself. We are not trying to use this study to enhance some other study or belief."

longer troubled. The entirety of Scientology auditing and the training of auditors is delineated by the Scientology Bridge which, in turn, describes a route to ever greater awareness and ability—whether, as Ron so provocatively phrased it, "the person remains a man or becomes something else."

How L. Ron Hubbard arrived at that statement and what it means within the larger context of our lives is, of course, the primary subject of all that is presented here. As a last introductory word, however, let us emphasize the principal themes. First, those who imagine a remote and contemplative philosopher are about to be disabused; for when we speak of Ron's philosophic journey, we are genuinely speaking of a *journey*—not a sifting of ideas in some academic cloister, but a study of existence from what he truthfully termed "the top down and the bottom up." Next, those who see this subject as largely irrelevant (or at best faintly interesting)

 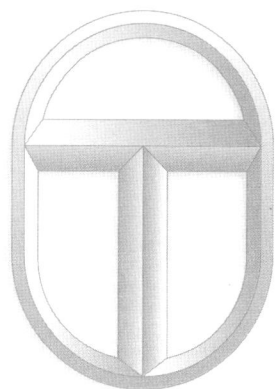

are about to be similarly disabused; for here is philosophy not as a discussion of life, but as a tool for life. In fact, here is philosophy as *life itself*. Finally, and particularly for those already familiar with the works of L. Ron Hubbard, here are various rare essays, selections and discussions from all critical junctures of Ron's philosophic path—from his earliest contemplative work, the now legendary "Excalibur," through a deeply personal "My Only Defense for Having Lived" to a never previously published conversation with renowned theologian Dr. Stillson Judah.

Additionally included are LRH notes on the phenomena of death, the revelation of past lives and our 1955 title piece, "The Rediscovery of the Human Soul," wherein he recounts a trek through what amounts to the whole of twentieth-century thought to finally arrive at what is a wholly extraordinary philosophic vista:

"We are studying the soul or spirit. We are studying it as itself. We are not trying to use this study to enhance some other study or belief. And we are telling the story of how it came about that the soul needed rediscovering." ■

CHAPTER ONE

A Note on
SURVIVE AND
"EXCALIBUR"

A Note on Survive and "Excalibur"

> "SUPPOSE ALL THE WISDOM OF THE WORLD *WERE* REDUCED TO just one line; suppose that one line were to be written today and given to you...." —L. Ron Hubbard

Long before the advent of either Dianetics or Scientology, those at all familiar with L. Ron Hubbard had come to expect he would eventually make a remarkable entrance into the philosophic realm. That entrance, largely conceived through the course of an extraordinary week in early 1938, is remembered today as "Excalibur." In the simplest terms, the work may be described as a first philosophic statement. Previously (and as we shall see in forthcoming articles) he had traveled far and established much as regards a philosophic foundation. Yet here, at the age of twenty-six, came his earliest formal summary, "to align my own ideas," as he modestly termed it, "for my own particular benefit." Given all the manuscript eventually inspired, however—two copies were actually stolen by agents of foreign intelligence services who wished to appropriate those ideas for political ends and only sections remain—such a description seems hardly enough.

At the core of "Excalibur" is Ron's revelatory statement on Survive as the single common denominator of existence. That all life forms are attempting to survive is, of course, a known datum. But that life is *only* attempting to survive—this was new. Moreover, how he interpreted the datum was new, i.e., a "finite measuring stick," as he elsewhere terms it, with which whole fields of knowledge might be coordinated. Those at all familiar with the works of Herbert Spencer (Ron himself apparently waded through at least the principal ten volumes of the *Synthetic Philosophy*) may recognize the concept:

"The proper field and function of philosophy lies in the summation and unification of the results of science. 'Knowledge of the lowest kind is un-unified knowledge; science is partially unified knowledge; philosophy is completely unified knowledge.' Such complete unification requires a broad and universal principle that will include all experience, and will describe

The L. Ron Hubbard home at Port Orchard, Washington, above Puget Sound. Here stood his legendary writer's retreat, also known as the "Hilltop Cabin" and where he authored a first philosophic work, remembered today as "Excalibur."

8 THE L. RON HUBBARD SERIES | *Philosopher & Founder*

Puget Sound, Washington: site of intense LRH research and discovery from 1937 to 1940

the essential features of all knowledge. Is there a principle of this kind?"

To which, of course, "Excalibur" replies unequivocally with *Survive!*

How Ron actually arrived at Survive is a fairly monumental story, but particularly involves a pivotal sequence of 1937 cytological experiments wherein he was able to demonstrate a cellularly inherited response to toxic substances. That is, having cultured a strain of bacterial cells, the culture was exposed to jets of steam, which affected the cells not at all. Next, applying jets of inherently toxic cigarette smoke, he keenly observed the culture both reacting and retreating from the threat. After continued "taunting" with smoke, he then substituted steam to observe the cells now misidentifying the steam as toxic and similarly retreating. Finally, culturing second and third generations of cells from the first, he found that when these later-generation cells were exposed to steam, they likewise misidentified the steam for toxic smoke and retreated in the name of survival.

If the point seems academic, it is not; for according to Darwinian theory, and hence the foundation of all biological and behavioral thought, learned responses cannot be inherited.

A Note on Survive and "Excalibur"

Rather, all life is said to be directed by chance, by a dumb roll of genetic dice as it were. Thus, for example, the ancestral bird develops wings purely as a biochemical function and not according to some inherent thrust towards survival. Yet the moment we introduce survival as a pervasive drive, passed on from cell to cell, we are introducing an *intelligence* behind the scheme of life—an "X factor," as Ron initially termed it, that shapes and gives meaning to life in ways that Darwin simply could not explain. As of those first weeks of 1938 and the drafting of his manuscript, Ron would say little more regarding this X factor. But in considering the central message of "Excalibur," he could not help but wonder who or what first gave that resounding one command, *Survive!*

Needless to say, the scope of "Excalibur" is immense and proposes not only the means of placing all life—be it human or cellular—into a definitive framework of Survive, but a method of resolving any problems related to existence. Or as Ron himself explains, "This book's design is to indicate the true perspective of a man's life." That "Excalibur" did not, however, also offer a workable therapy was the principal reason Ron finally chose not to publish the manuscript. That is, if the whole of his quest may be defined in terms of a conviction that philosophy must be workable, must be capable of application, then "Excalibur" could only be regarded as a steppingstone. Nevertheless, with the eventual development of Dianetics, all that is essentially "Excalibur" was made public and, in fact, may be found in *Dianetics: The Modern Science of Mental Health* and *Dianetics: The Original Thesis*.

Presented here are the opening pages of "Excalibur." As an additional word, it might be mentioned that all events recounted here took place in Ron's Port Orchard, Washington, cabin—except, of course, Ron's prefatory note on his near-fatal operation at the Bremerton, Washington, dental office of Dr. Elbert E. Cone... ■

> *"Suppose all the wisdom of the world were reduced to just one line; suppose that one line were to be written today and given to you."*

Port Orchard, Washington
January 1, 1938

It began with an operation. I took gas as an anesthetic and while under the influence of it my heart must have stopped beating, as in my terror I knew I was slipping through the Curtain and into the land of shades. It was like sliding helter-skelter down into a vortex of scarlet and it was knowing that one was dying and that the process of dying was far from pleasant. For a long time after I knew that "Death is eight inches below life." It was terrible work, climbing up out of the cone again, for Something did not want to let me back through the wall, and then, when I willed my going, I determined it against all opposition. And Something began to cry out, "Don't let him know!" and then fainter, "Don't let him know."

Though badly shaken I was quite rational when I was restored. The people around me looked frightened—more frightened than I. I was not thinking about what I had been through nearly so much as what I *knew*. I had not yet fully returned to life. I was still in contact with Something. And in that state I remained for some days, all the while puzzling over what I *knew*. It was clear that if I could but remember I would have the secret of life. This in itself was enough to drive one mad, so illusive was that just-beyond-reach information. And then one morning, just as I awoke, it came to me. I climbed out of my tall ship's bunk and made my way to my typewriter. I began to hammer out that secret and when I had written ten thousand words, then I knew even more clearly. I destroyed the ten thousand and began to write again.

EXCALIBUR

By

Ronald Hubbard

I

THE LOST KEY

Once upon a time, according to a writer in the Arabian
been — who made it the work of his life to collect all the wisdom
in the world. He wrote an enormous and learned volume, setting
forth everything he had found and, at last, sat back contented
with

JANUARY 1938

EXCALIBUR

by L. Ron Hubbard

Once upon a time, according to a writer in the *Arabian Nights,* there lived a very wise old man—and wise he must have been—who made it the work of his life to collect all the wisdom in the world. He wrote an enormous and learned volume, setting forth everything he had found and, at last, sat back contented with a task well done. Presently, his contentment was dissipated by the thought that he had written too much. So he sat himself down for ten years more and reduced the original volume to one a tenth its size.

When he had finished, he again thought himself content, but again discovered he was wrong. With painstaking exactitude, he reduced this second work to a single page. Another ten years passed and the ancient philosopher grew even wiser. He took that single page and reduced it to just a single line which contained everything there was to be known. A decade more found the old scribe close to death. He had placed that remarkable line in a niche in the wall for safekeeping, intending to tell his son about it. But now he changed his mind once more.

He tore up even that line.

Suppose all the wisdom of the world *were* reduced to just one line; suppose that one line were to be written today and given to you. With it you could

understand the basis of all life and endeavor: love, politics, war, friendship, criminality, insanity, history, business, religion, kings, cats, society, art, mythology, your children, communism, bankers, sailors, tigers and other matters without end. More: suppose this one line could tell you all about yourself, could solve all your problems, quiet your restlessness.

If all the wisdom of the world could be compressed into a single line, certainly it would do all these things and more. There *is* one line, conjured up out of a morass of facts and made available as an integrated unit to explain such things. This line is the philosophy of philosophy, thereby carrying the entire subject back into the simple and humble truth.

All life is directed by one command and one command only—SURVIVE!

EXCALIBUR

By

Ronald Hubbard

I

THE LOST KEY

Once upon a time, according to a writer in the Arabian
lived a very wise old man — and wise he must have
it the work of his life to collect all the wisdom
wrote an enormous and learned volume, setting
had found and, at last, sat back contented
Presently, his contentment was dissipated
had written too much. So he sat himself
and reduced the original volume to one

ed, he again thought himself content,
wrong. With painstaking exactitude,

Hilltop writer's retreat at Port Orchard, Washington

"I am sitting here in my cedar-lined cabin, where I have so many times sat, thundering away on my typewriter, digging into my books or gazing into yesterday or tomorrow."

—*L. Ron Hubbard*

By July 1938, with "Excalibur" on the shelf for want of a workable technology, Ron returned to his literary life in New York City. It was a heady time and chiefly remembered for his first works of speculative fiction on behalf of John W. Campbell, Jr.'s *Astounding Science Fiction*. Not, however, generally remembered is the fact Ron's initial effort only tangentially qualified as science fiction. More accurately, it was a work of philosophic fiction and drawn from the same deep well as "Excalibur."

It was entitled "The Dangerous Dimension." The protagonist is a professor of philosophy who stumbles on an arcane formula that teleports him to any locale he envisions—New York, Paris, Mars and, inevitably, the Sun. While Ron himself admitted the work lacked any real scientific grounding, the philosophic foundation was indeed firm. Accordingly, and specifically to satisfy requests from readers, Ron provided "Tomorrow's Miracles."

It is prefaced with a simple statement of particulars.

"The background of the 'Dangerous Dimension' is philosophic. It is quite authentic. The Veda, Yogism, long, long ago found its first cheela going into a trance from which he could project himself, the life essence of himself, into far realms and ranges. This Indian basis is quite valid when one considers that all our religions and a great deal of our science has wandered in from India, and that is part of a vast creed."

Also among his prefatory notes is a word on Anglo-Irish philosopher George Berkeley (1685–1753), who maintained "All is a divine intelligence," which in turn harkened back to an ancient idea that "Everything is a Mind and therefore there exists nothing but Mind and, hence, no space." There is still more again on cryptic formulations of Spinoza and the principles of Spencer. But the long and short is merely Ron's abiding question: Was speculative science, in fact, but a stepchild of Eastern philosophy? And if so: "Was it science at all? Or was it something else, even greater?"

In what amounts to Ron's summary statement on all philosophic thinking, then, we present "Tomorrow's Miracles."

LATE 1938

TOMORROW'S MIRACLES

by L. Ron Hubbard

How many men have ever paused in the summer night to look up at the stars and give a thought, not to astronomy, but to the men who first slashed the Gordian knot of planetary motion? Of course all educated men have, at one time or another, scraped the surface of the source of such facts. But today we speak grandly of galaxies and consider astronomy an exact science and bow down before facts.

There probably does not exist a professor in the world who has not, unwittingly or otherwise, held the ignorance of the ancients to ridicule; and there is no field where this is more apparent than astronomy.

Some of the facts are these:

> Early Hebrews and Chaldeans, among others, believed in a flat earth, a sky supported by mountains and which upheld a sea, which, in turn, leaked through and caused rain. The flat plain was supported by nothing in particular. Of course we all know this, but there is a worthwhile point to make.
>
> The Hindus believed that the earth was a hemisphere, supported by four large elephants. "This seems to have been entirely satisfactory until someone asked what was holding the elephants up. After some discussion, the wise men of India agreed that the four elephants were standing on a large mud turtle. Again the people seem to have been satisfied until some inquisitive person raised the question as to what was holding the mud turtle up. I imagine the philosophers had grown tired of

answering these questions by this time, for they are said to have replied that there was mud under the mud turtle and mud all the rest of the way."*

Twelve pillars, according to the Veda of India, supported the earth, leaving plenty of room for the sun and the moon to dive under and come up on the other side.

If you wish, you can find a multitude of such beliefs, all common enough. But there are two facts concerning these and their presentation which are most erroneous. By examining the above quote one sees that terms have been confused. Men who ask questions and then figure out answers are, indeed, philosophers. The masses take anything which seems to have a certain academic reverence attached and cling to it desperately. Priests, not philosophers, satisfy the masses, which led Schopenhauer to call religion the "metaphysics of the masses." The other error is considering that these beliefs were foolish and that scientists, laboring in their laboratories or observatories, are wholly responsible for the ideas which permeate the world of thought.

It is not that we here wish to maintain these facts about the state of the earth. On the contrary. But they are not presented for ridicule, because they are the ideas which some philosopher developed painfully with the scant data he had at hand and who had, to aid him, no means of communication, travel, instruments or even mathematics. They are, what we chose to call, hypotheses possessing sufficient truth to be accepted. Today, thanks to Copernicus and all the rest, we know about gravity. Thanks to Newton we have mathematics. Thanks to a lens grinder we have a telescope.

It was stated in an early Sanscrit treatise that the world is round. Thales, Homer, Aristotle, Pythagoras, Ptolemy and others conceived various evidences which demonstrated that the earth was a sphere. In 250 B.C. Eratosthenes computed the earth's circumference, missing it only by one hundred miles (and he had no mechanical aids or "higher" mathematics).

Of course these gentlemen made errors in their hypotheses. Ptolemy, 140 B.C., conceived of seven crystalline spheres to account for planetary motion. To counter this, long before (in the sixth century B.C.), Pythagoras taught that the earth went around the sun but erred in supposing the sun to be the center of the universe. Aristarchus, in the third century B.C. and Capella in the fifth century A.D., also taught that the earth revolved, itself, and around the sun. Copernicus, in the sixteenth century, gave the world the system which is now used.

Now the point we wish to make is this: Down through the ages men have conceived various hypotheses with regard to astronomy. Concurrently, instruments were invented and other discoveries made and into the hands of investigators was placed a complete idea plus the means of examining it. There has been considerable lag, naturally, between widespread belief and philosophic location of new truths.

We are fond of thinking in terms of tomorrow. But the future is written with the pen of the present in the ink of the past. We are fond of believing that that which we now possess is infallible and not subject to any great change. And, when we begin to localize certain fields for investigation, science feeds wholly upon the statements of predecessors. Should a man put forth

---

Astronomy by Arthur M. Harding, PhD, p. 4

a new theory (there hasn't been one since the nineteenth century), then he is no longer a scientist but a philosopher.

Let us remember our Voltaire and his admonition to define our terms. What is science? What is philosophy? Further, by knowing, what can we hope to gain by it? Will we benefit enough to talk about it? The answer to the last two is definitely yes.

To quote Spencer, "Knowledge of the lowest kind is un-unified knowledge; science is partially unified knowledge; philosophy is completely unified knowledge."*

Philosophy is *not* the muttering of epigrams nor is the true philosopher merely one who can quote at random from various great works.

> "We are fond of thinking in terms of tomorrow. But the future is written with the pen of the present in the ink of the past."

Consider an explorer, casting away, all too often, his greatest securities, even his life, to stride forward into the outer dark, throwing up his star shells to view what lies in the unknown. He lacks a vocabulary suitable to record his findings because the words have yet to be invented. He lacks instruments to measure what he thinks he sees because no instruments for such are yet in existence. He stumbles and trips, pushing ever outward on his lonely track, farther and farther from the milestoned roads where statements are safe and conversants many. He is so far out that those in their safe, warm homes of "proved thought" cannot recognize the distance he has traversed when he first covers it.

His is the task of stabbing deeper into the Unknown and the dangers he runs are those of ridicule. He knows, in his heart of hearts, what his fate will most likely be. He may come back with some great idea only to find that men laugh. He may point a road which will be a thoroughfare within a century, but men, having but little vision, see only a tangle of undergrowth and blackness beyond and push but timidly where the first to go pushed forward with such courage.

In all the ages of history, thinking men have been crucified either by institutions or the masses. But those very ideas which at first seemed so mad and impossible are those which science now uses to polish up its reputation.

Inevitably, the philosopher, the true searcher, is decried. But then, it is perfectly natural. His breadth of view is so great and penetrating that he can unify all of the knowledge groups, taking his findings to discover a lower common denominator.

It is quite natural that he should do this, just as it is that his work should usually be spurned by his own generation.

Un-unified knowledge is that possessed by every animal or drudge. "A cake of soap cleans a shirt." "A cake of soap cleans a floor." "A cake of soap cleans the face."

Partially unified knowledge on the subject would be: "A cake of soap cleans" and "Let us see how many things a cake of soap will clean."

Completely unified knowledge on the subject would be: "Any agent which holds foreign matter in solution will clean."

First Principles, p. 103

The argument here is quite plain. Partially unified knowledge has become a group of men all anxious to assemble data on the science of soap. The completely unified knowledge opens up a new vista, the possibility of discovering some medium which will clean anything.

And if you think this is facetious, know that there is no medium which will clean everything and anything equally well. It would be essentially destructive to a million volumes of hard-won data concerning soap. The philosopher has come up against a resistant force. He reduced the matter to simplicity and indicated that it was necessary to search for a new cleaner, not a new method. Put into practice immediately and, meeting with success, the idea would destroy, for instance, the business of hundreds of soap factories and would, of course, throw umpteen thousand soap chemists out of excellent jobs.

> *"Philosophy is not the muttering of epigrams nor is the true philosopher merely one who can quote at random from various great works."*

There is nothing being used today except those ideas given to the world by philosophers. For instance, Spinoza is responsible for most of modern psychology. Plato wrote about psychoanalysis in his *Republic* (in addition to most of our ideas on the political side of the ledger as well). Anaximander (610–540 B.C.) outlined our theory of evolution and Empedocles (445 B.C.) developed it as far as we have gone, originating natural selection. Democritus said, "In reality there are only atoms and the void" and went on to outline the theories of planetary evolution much as they are used today. The Ionian Greeks developed the major portion of our physics. Kant handed out the finishing touches, with Schopenhauer (a strange combination, this) on our psychology, Spencer on evolution; Newton put natural laws into equations and invented mathematics to work them. Spinoza went so far into the realm of the outer dark that no one has caught up to him yet, though the trails are being followed slowly and inexorably to the destinations he indicated. But science in each case contemporarily taught and used outworn systems and considered that it had reached an outer frontier when, in reality, science was always hundreds of years behind the philosophic frontier!

In short, science has the unhealthy tendency to isolate and expand that isolation, where philosophy tends to reach higher or more general laws. Give a scientist a theory (witness cytology) and he immediately sets out and collects gravitically all the facts pertinent to that one thing. To the scientist is owed the particulars. The scientist inherits the theories and instruments already conceived and smooths out the rough spots. The philosopher is challenged because he does not do this, but, as we have remarked, he has no instruments, no tables, no aid of any kind which has reached as far as he has gone forward.

In this manner, science tends to group and then complicate any subject. It is to science that the masses owe their benefits. It is to the philosopher that science owes all its fuel. The citizen, seeing not very far, praises where praise is really due, but not wholly due, to the point where a scientist can laugh at philosophic ideas, the very things which gave him the material with which to work.

That science does attempt to propagandize its importance to the extent of origination is attested by the commonly heard statement that "Now everything is all invented and if one would desire fame, he must specialize." That word *specialize* is a red flag to any philosopher because it automatically indicates the localizing of knowledge into hideous complexities which, he knows very well, will be destroyed just as all other complicated structures were ripped down when a new truth was isolated. Now it is indicative of the essential nature of science that it wars ceaselessly within itself in favor of this or that hypothesis as countering another hypothesis. It can be said with truth that the battles of philosophy are fought by science against science. Science comes along with measuring sticks of the already known, takes sides and begins to fire, without once inventing any substitute or new hypotheses of its own and ridiculing any which may be offered. So stubborn is science that it hangs to its achieved tomes like a bulldog. Ptolemy's weird theory of crystalline spheres was taught currently with the revised Copernican system in one of the oldest American universities for many years.

"It is to science that the masses owe their benefits. It is to the philosopher that science owes all its fuel."

This is no diatribe against science, it is a defense of new theories, new ideas, new concepts and the men who make them. The laughter leveled at the heads of innovators is amusing only if it be remembered that the ideas now in use were once equally ridiculed by science. And one has only to glance back with the perspective of the years to see that science has embraced many things much more weird—such as a hemisphere on four elephants on a mud turtle on mud, mud, mud. Doubtless, in this instance, there were a hundred libraries filled with tracts to the effect that the mud turtle had green eyes as against the opinion of another that his eyes were purple. Basing this on horizon stars and examining them as reflection, scientists of that day were likely very learned within their sphere of findings.

But there is such a thing as a cumulation of knowledge. By this most men envision being swamped by facts and books. Libraries crammed to the roof, laboratories humming, men shouting in lecture rooms, men writing vast discourses on electrons and positrons..... But there is no need for alarm. Ten times as much data has been stacked away in the basement, where it molds forgotten, the product of but fifty years ago but now disproved through the scientific acceptance of higher generalizations. Each time a higher generalization is reached, all men shout, "This is the ULTIMATE! Man can go no farther!" But they forget that in quiet places men are looking all about them, not at one special object, but at all objects and so it comes as a shock when a perfectly simple truth which was right under everybody's nose all the time was brought to light.

Just as God's connection with Man and the Creator of the Universe (Prime Mover Unmoved or whatever God might really be) is pushed back step by step infinitely, so is all knowledge simplified.

Two hundred years ago (although it had probably been outlined already) science would have blinked at the idea of splitting the atom. Science dealt in atoms and molecules in that day and nothing smaller. Today every schoolboy knows that an atom can be split and remade into several things. A hundred years from now men will look back at this atom splitting and shake their heads over such stupidity as thinking that an electron was the smallest division.

But how do we get to the point where we can look back? The answer is somewhere in our midst. Just who will advance the theory and method for releasing atomic energy is not important. That the possibility of doing so has been often cited and that various means are constantly being proposed is the course which will lead to such a thing. And do not for one hypnotized moment suppose that the method will be born in any flashing, sparking laboratory endowed with millions. On the contrary. It will first be proposed by a thinker. The laboratory may later claim all the credit, but that is of no matter, it seems, as long as men can then begin to write all about the mathematics of disintegration with which they will fill ten thousand libraries.

If this cannot be believed, if it cannot be accepted that all truths are simple truths and need only to be pointed out, recall that the splitting of the atom was a simple truth. Then, if it be a matter of concern that the only discoveries left will be complex and that specialization is paramount, remember that the discovery of the disintegration of the atom will scrap all the fine tomes (which fill ten thousand libraries) on the subject of internal-combustion engines and propelling forces in general as well as all extant hull, wheel and wing designs. The only thing of these fine flights which will remain is the essential truth from which they were born.

Knowledge is not a swamping sea of facts, but a long line of simple truths, each one more simple than the last. If one would discover the next in line, let him not in any specialized field, but rather in a cross between two fields or more. And as a man cannot be specialized in half a dozen fields it remains that his investigations would have to be wholly independent of any rubber-stamped outlook. The atom disintegrator may come as a cross between botany and physics. Who would dream of such a thing? But already the newest source of energy is the leaf of a tree. Would a physicist, interested only in physics, have discovered that? It is doubtful. He would have to be more concerned with the entire world around him than he would be with his immediate laboratory bench. Strangely

enough, the men who have isolated the greatest truths have not been what is generally known as "an educated man." Widely read, yes. Intelligent, certainly. But above all, anxious to push into anything and everything where the devil would fear to tread.

This thirst for adventure into the abstract is the motivating force of all youth. Later, weighed down with admonitions that one must specialize, youth succumbs to the lure of security and forgets about those things he wanted to plan, in the scramble to read all everybody ever said on the subject of Trimming Frogs' Toenails.

To be very specific, today the scientist mocks wild ideas about interplanetary travel, saying, "Welllll, yess, it might be done....maybe. But.........." With all respect to him he is perfectly right. He has a certain job of his own to do. He will probably be dead long before Man first sets foot on the moon. But that the dream, any wildest dream, can be accomplished needs only the verification of the source of most of our mechanical marvels today. Submarine? Locomotive? Airplane? Stratosphere and overweather? Typewriter? Traffic signals? Look at what you may and where you may, you will uncover "science fiction" or a man interested in it.

The philosophers of the great general ideas are, of course, in a class by themselves. But as far as the advanced applications of various methods and hybrid sciences, as far as the forecast of our civilization and, indeed, our very architecture of tomorrow, one has only to search the files.

> *"Knowledge is not a swamping sea of facts, but a long line of simple truths, each one more simple than the last."*

Men have been writing "science fiction" since the Phoenicians, perhaps. At least the first story followed soon after writing itself. Once where the "pseudo" "science" sent a man west on an iron horse to fight Indians (which didn't happen really until many, many years had flown), it now sends men into the outer galaxies.

Among the scientists of today are many outlaws, not quite philosophers, but still intrigued by the ideas which can be turned up.

Looking back into the past's dim depths one can see a great many "foolish" ideas brought to fruition. Looking ahead into the future, one can see..............

Men have been writing "science-fiction" since the Phoenicians, perhaps. At least the first story followed soon after writing itself. Once where the "pseudo" "science" sent a man west on an iron horse to fight Indians (which didn't happen really until many, many years had flown), it now sends men into the outer galaxies.

Among the scientists of today are many outlaws, not quite philosophers, but still intrigued by the ideas which can be turned up.

Looking back into the past's dim depths one can see a great many "foolish" ideas brought to fruition............. Looking ahead into the future, one can see—

CHAPTER TWO

The Birth of
DIANETICS

The Birth of Dianetics

FOR SIX INTERMITTENT YEARS BEYOND 1938, RON CONTINUED his examination of Survive to effectively determine if more could be derived, extrapolated or discerned. Of special note along this track was his 1940 expedition to Northwest Coast Indian lands off British Columbia and his examination of mythology as a vehicle for cultural

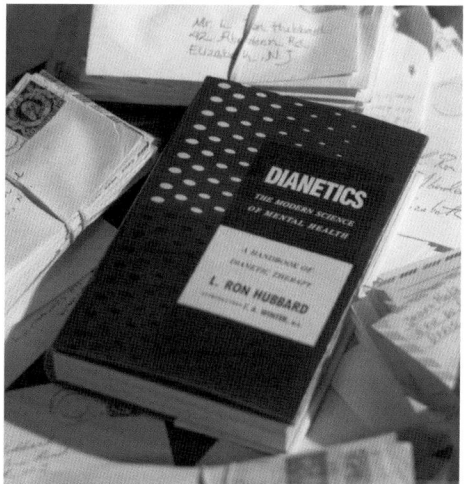

survival; in particular, the myth as a means of perpetuating a tribal identity. He had also grown quite fascinated with those myths apparently rooted in actual events, e.g., the near-universal deluge myth arguably inspired by dim memories from the end of the last Ice Age. Yet in the main, and particularly with the advent of the Second World War, the emphasis lay on practicality. That is, what in the way of an actual therapy could one also derive from Survive?

The answer was, of course, Dianetics, but the route was a tortuous one and finally led through a good deal more: an exhaustive examination of all psychoanalytic theory, an extensive review of then current neural theory, still more cellular study and a series of extraordinary tests on links between hypnosis and insanity. Yet if we are to only retrace the milestones, then our next step lies in the recovery ward of an Oak Knoll Naval Hospital, where then Lieutenant L. Ron Hubbard spent the better part of eight months through 1945.

Specifically at issue was the fate of fifteen former prisoners of Japanese internment camps, who, after near-starvation diets through the course of confinement, were found unable to assimilate protein. Even with intensive

Elizabeth, New Jersey, 1950

> *"Dianetics is an exact science and its application is on the order of, but simpler than, engineering. Its axioms should not be confused with theories since they demonstrably exist as natural laws hitherto undiscovered."*

testosterone treatment, generally effective in thousands of such cases, these unfortunate fifteen essentially continued to starve. In reply, and after extensive scrutiny of the endocrinological link to protein assimilation, LRH proposed a crucial theory: "If the mind regulated the body and not the body regulated the mind," he explained, "then the endocrine system would not respond to hormones if there was in existence a mental block." Whereupon he proceeded with the first formal application of early Dianetics techniques, and so literally saved the lives of those fifteen former prisoners. He also derived a genuinely landmark formulation—specifically that thought took precedence over the physical... Or as he so famously phrased it: "Function monitors structure."

Presented here is what ultimately followed from that central revelation at Oak Knoll: *Dianetics: The Modern Science of Mental Health* and, in particular, the opening synopsis of that work as originally provided friends and colleagues in advance of publication. In a word, this was the piece through which Ron originally introduced Dianetics to those who simply could not wait for a book in hand. To wit:

"Had I had any time to breathe I would have used it to say hello in person. But I haven't. The enclosed synopsis will tell you why."

This is also the piece with which he originally sparked a Dianetics firestorm among American literati. Hence, his terse but telling note to Southern California's contingent from the *Astounding* stable:

"This synopsis makes you the West Coast authority!"

That Ron specifically directed his reader's attention to the greater philosophic background woven through the piece is more than a little significant. For albeit only touched on and albeit highly distilled, here indeed is the essence of what he described as a Dianetics philosophy that "solves a lot more riddles than mental ills and ailments." ∎

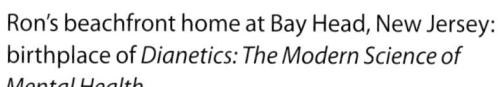

Ron's beachfront home at Bay Head, New Jersey: birthplace of *Dianetics: The Modern Science of Mental Health*

```
                    DIANETICS:
          THE MODERN SCIENCE OF MENTAL HEALTH



                         by



                   L. Ron Hubbard




              BOOK ONE, CHAPTER ONE
```

A SYNOPSIS OF DIANETICS

by L. Ron Hubbard

Dianetics (Greek *dia,* through, and *nous,* mind or soul) is the science of mind. Far simpler than physics or chemistry, it compares with them in the exactness of its axioms and is on a considerably higher echelon of usefulness. *The hidden source of all psychosomatic ills and human aberration has been discovered and skills have been developed for their invariable cure.*

DIANETICS IS ACTUALLY A family of sciences embracing the various humanities and translating them into usefully precise definitions. The present volume deals with Individual Dianetics and is a handbook containing the necessary skills both for the handling of interpersonal relations and the treatment of the mind. With the techniques presented in this handbook, the intelligent layman can successfully treat all psychosomatic ills and inorganic aberrations. More importantly, the skills offered in this handbook will produce the Dianetic *Clear,* an optimum individual with intelligence considerably greater than the current normal, or the Dianetic *Release,* an individual who has been freed from his major anxieties or illnesses. The Release can be done in less than twenty hours of work and is a state superior to any produced by several years of psychoanalysis, since the Release will not relapse.

Dianetics is an exact science and its application is on the order of, but simpler than, engineering. Its axioms should not be confused with theories since they demonstrably exist as natural laws hitherto undiscovered. Man has known many portions of Dianetics in the past thousands of years, but the data was not evaluated for importance, was not organized into a body of precise knowledge. In addition to things known if not evaluated, Dianetics includes a large number of new discoveries of its own about thought and the mind.

The axioms may be found on the end sheets of this volume.* Understood and applied, they embrace the field of human endeavor and thought and yield precision results.

Below
The original insignia of Dianetics

In reference to Dianetics: The Modern Science of Mental Health, where this synopsis appears.

The first contribution of Dianetics is the discovery that the problems of thought and mental function can be resolved within the bounds of the finite universe, which is to say that all data needful to the solution of mental action and Man's endeavor can be measured, sensed and experienced as scientific truths independent of mysticism or metaphysics. The various axioms are not assumptions or theories—the case of past ideas about the mind—but are laws which can be subjected to the most vigorous laboratory and clinical tests.

The first law of Dianetics is a statement of the Dynamic Principle of Existence.

THE DYNAMIC PRINCIPLE OF EXISTENCE IS: SURVIVE!

No behavior or activity has been found to exist without this principle. It is not new that life is surviving. It is new that life has as its entire dynamic urge *only* survival.

Survival is divided into four dynamics. Survival can be understood to lie in any one of the dynamics and by faulty logic can be explained in terms of any one dynamic. A man can be said to survive for self alone and by this all behavior can be formulated. He can be said to survive for sex alone and by sex alone all behavior can be formulated. He can be said to survive for the group only or for Mankind only, and in either of these the entire endeavor and behavior of the individual can be equated and explained. These are four equations of survival, each one apparently true. However, the entire problem of the purpose of Man cannot be resolved unless one admits all four dynamics in each individual. So equated, the behavior of the individual can be estimated with precision. These dynamics then embrace the activity of one or many men.

> **DYNAMIC ONE:** The urge of the individual to reach the highest potential of survival in terms of *self* and his immediate symbiotes.
>
> **DYNAMIC TWO:** The urge of the individual to reach the highest potential of survival in terms of *sex,* the act and the creation of children and their rearing.
>
> **DYNAMIC THREE:** The urge of the individual to reach the highest potential of survival in terms of the *group,* whether civil, political, or racial and the symbiotes of that group.
>
> **DYNAMIC FOUR:** The urge of the individual to reach the highest potential of survival in terms of *Mankind* and the symbiotes of Mankind.

Thus motivated, the individual or a society seeks survival and no human activity of any kind has other basis: experiment, investigation and long testing demonstrated that the *unaberrated individual,* the Clear, was motivated in his actions and decisions by *all* the above dynamics and not one alone.

The Clear, the goal of Dianetic therapy, can be created from psychotic, neurotic, deranged, criminal or normal people if they have organically sound nervous systems. He demonstrates the basic nature of Mankind and that basic nature has been found uniformly and invariably to be *good.* That is now an established *scientific fact,* not an opinion.

The Clear has attained a stable state on a very high plane. He is persistent and vigorous and pursues life with enthusiasm and satisfaction. He is motivated by the four dynamics as above. He has attained the full power and use of hitherto hidden abilities.

The inhibition of one or more dynamics in an individual causes an aberrated condition, tends toward mental derangement and psychosomatic illness and causes the individual to make irrational conclusions and act, still in an effort to survive, in destructive ways.

Dianetic technique deletes, without drugs, hypnotism, surgery, shock or other artificial means, the blocks from these various dynamics. The removal of these blocks permits the free flow of the various dynamics and, of course, results in a heightened persistency in life and a much higher intelligence.

The precision of Dianetics makes it possible to impede or release these dynamics at will with invariable results.

"The hidden source of all inorganic mental disturbance and psychosomatic illness was one of the discoveries of Dianetics. This source had been unknown and unsuspected, though vigorously sought, for thousands of years."

The hidden source of all inorganic mental disturbance and psychosomatic illness was one of the discoveries of Dianetics. This source had been unknown and unsuspected, though vigorously sought, for thousands of years. That the discovered source *is* the source requires less laboratory proof than would have been necessary to have proven the correctness of William Harvey's discovery of the circulation of the blood. The proof does not depend upon a laboratory test with complicated apparatus, but can be made in any group of men by any intelligent individual.

The *source of aberration* has been found to be a hitherto unsuspected sub-mind which, complete with its own recordings, underlies what Man understands to be his "conscious" mind. The concept of the unconscious mind is replaced in Dianetics by the discovery that the "unconscious" mind is the *only* mind which is *always* conscious. In Dianetics this sub-mind is called the *reactive mind.* A holdover from an earlier step in Man's evolution, the reactive mind possesses vigor and command power on a cellular level. It does not "remember": it records and uses the recordings only to produce action. It does not "think": it selects recordings and impinges them upon the "conscious" mind and the body without the knowledge or consent of the individual. The only information the individual has of such action is his occasional perception that he is not acting rationally about one thing or another and cannot understand why. There is no "censor."

The reactive mind operates exclusively on physical pain and painful emotion. It is not capable of differentiative thought, but acts on the stimulus-response basis. This is the principle on which the animal mind functions. It does not receive its recordings as memory or experience, but only as forces to be reactivated. It receives its recordings as cellular *engrams* when the "conscious" mind is "unconscious."

In a drugged state, when anesthetized as in an operation, when rendered "unconscious" by injury or illness, the individual yet has his reactive mind in full operation. He may not be "aware" of what has

Dianetics: A study of the mind—fastest

WED., SEPT. 6, 1950 · DAILY NEWS, LOS ANGELES · 2

L. RON HUBBARD LAUGHS READILY
Because "Dianetics is no solemn adventure"

HE EXPLAINS, DOES NOT DEFEND
"A science of mind was a goal…of Man"

Above
The *Dianetics* author as presented in a six-part series published by the *Los Angeles Daily News,* September 1950

taken place, but, as Dianetics has discovered and can prove, everything which happened to him in the interval of "unconsciousness" was fully and completely recorded. This information is unappraised by his conscious mind, neither evaluated nor reasoned. It can, at any future date, become reactivated by similar circumstances observed by the awake and conscious individual. When any such recording, an engram, becomes reactivated, it has command power. It shuts down the conscious mind to greater or lesser degree, takes over the motor controls of the body and causes behavior and action to which the conscious mind, the individual himself, would never consent. He is, nevertheless, handled like a marionette by his engrams.

The antagonistic forces of the exterior environment thus become entered into the individual himself without the knowledge or consent of the individual. And there they create an interior world of force which exerts itself not only against the exterior world, but against the individual himself. Aberration is caused by what has been done *to,* not done *by* the individual.

Man has unwittingly long aided the reactive mind by supposing that a person, when "unconscious" from drugs, illness, injury or anesthetic, had no recording ability. This permits an enormous amount

growing "movement" in America

ALL OF LIFE WAS FASCINATING
"I began to think of men as basic units"

RESEARCH WAS HIS INSTRUMENT
"I knew what the principles were but…"

of data to enter into the reactive bank since none have been careful to maintain silence around an "unconscious" person. The invention of language and the entrance of language into the engram bank of the reactive mind seriously complicates the mechanistic reactions. The engrams containing language impinge themselves upon the conscious mind as commands. Engrams then contain command value much higher than any in the exterior world. Thought is directed and motivated by the irrational engrams. Thought processes are disturbed not only by these engramic commands, but also by the fact that the reactive mind reduces, by regenerating unconsciousness, the actual ability to think. Few people possess, because of this, more than 10 percent of their potential awareness.

The entire physical pain and painful emotion of a lifetime—whether the individual "knows" about it or not—is contained, recorded, in the engram bank. Nothing is forgotten. And all physical pain and painful emotion, no matter how the individual may think he has handled it, is capable of re-inflicting itself upon him from this hidden level unless that pain is removed by Dianetic therapy.

The engram and only the engram causes aberration and psychosomatic illness.

Dianetic therapy may be briefly stated. Dianetics deletes all the pain from a lifetime. When this pain is erased in the engram bank and refiled as memory and experience in the memory banks, all aberrations and psychosomatic illnesses vanish, the dynamics are entirely rehabilitated and the physical and mental being regenerate. Dianetics leaves an individual full memory, but without pain. Exhaustive tests have demonstrated that hidden pain is not a necessity, but is invariably and *always* a liability to the health, skill, happiness and survival potential of the individual. It has *no* survival value.

The method which is used to refile pain is another discovery. Man has unknowingly possessed another process of remembering of which he has not been cognizant. Here and there a few have known about it and used it without realizing what they did or that they did something which Man as a whole did not know could be done. This process is *returning*. Wide awake and without drugs an individual can *return* to any period of his entire life providing his passage is not blocked by engrams. Dianetics developed techniques for circumventing these blocks and reducing them from the status of Powerful Unknown to useful memory.

> *"The completeness and profusion of data in the standard banks is a discovery of Dianetics, and the significance of such recalls is yet another discovery."*

The technique of therapy is done in what is called a Dianetic *reverie*. The individual undergoing this process sits or lies in a quiet room accompanied by a friend or professional therapist who acts as *auditor*. The auditor directs the attention of the patient to the patient's self and then begins to place the patient in various periods of the patient's life merely by telling him to "go there" rather than "remember."

All therapy is done, not by remembering or associating, but by travel on the *time track*. Every human being has a time track. It begins with life and it ends with death. It is a sequence of events complete from portal to portal, as recorded.

The conscious mind, in Dianetics, is called by the somewhat more precise term of *analytical mind*. The analytical mind consists of the "I" (the center of awareness), all computational ability of the individual and the standard memory banks—which are filled with all past perceptions of the individual, awake or normally asleep (all material which is not engramic). No data are missing from these standard banks, all are there, barring physical organic defects, in full motion, color, sound, tactile, smell and all other senses. The "I" may not be able to reach his standard banks because of reactive data which bar portions of the standard banks from the view of "I". Cleared, "I" is able to reach all moments of his lifetime without exertion or discomfort and perceive all he has ever sensed, recalling them in full motion, color, sound, tone and other senses. The completeness and profusion of data in the standard banks is a discovery of Dianetics, and the significance of such recalls is yet another discovery.

The auditor directs the travel of "I" along the patient's time track. The patient knows everything which is taking place, is in full control of himself and is able to bring himself to the present whenever he likes. No hypnotism or other means are used. Man may not have known he could do this, but it is simple.

The auditor, with precision methods, recovers data from the earliest "unconscious" moments of the patient's life, such "unconsciousness" being understood to be caused by shock or pain, not mere unawareness. The patient thus contacts the cellular-level engrams. Returned to them and progressed through them by the auditor, the patient re-experiences these moments a few times, when they are then erased and refiled automatically as standard memory. So far as the auditor and the patient can discover, the entire incident has now vanished and does not exist. If they searched carefully in the standard banks, they would find it again, but refiled as "Once aberrative, do not permit as such into computer." Late areas of "unconsciousness" are impenetrable until early ones are erased.

The amount of discomfort experienced by the patient is minor. He is repelled mainly by engramic commands which variously dictate emotion and reaction.

In a *Release,* the case is not progressed to the point of complete recall. In a *Clear,* full memory exists throughout the lifetime, with the additional bonus that he has photographic recall in color, motion, sound, etc., as well as optimum computational ability.

The psychosomatic illnesses of the *Release* are reduced, ordinarily, to a level where they do not thereafter trouble him. In a *Clear,* psychosomatic illness has become non-existent and will not return since its actual source is nullified permanently.

The Dianetic *Release* is comparable to a current normal or above. The Dianetic *Clear* is to a current normal individual as the current normal is to the severely insane.

Dianetics elucidates various problems with its many discoveries, its axioms, its organization and its technique. In the progress of its development many astonishing data were thrust upon it, for when one deals with natural laws and measurable actualities which produce specific and invariable results, one must accept what Nature holds, not what is pleasing or desired. When one deals with facts rather than theories and gazes for the first time upon the mechanisms of human action, several things confound him, much as the flutterings of the heart did Harvey or the actions of yeasts did Pasteur. The blood did not circulate because Harvey said it could nor yet because he said it did. It circulated and had been circulating for eons. Harvey was clever and observant enough to find it, and this was much the case with Pasteur and other explorers of the hitherto unknown or unconfirmed.

In Dianetics, the fact that the analytical mind was inherently *perfect* and remained structurally capable of restoration to full operation was not the least of the data found. That Man was good, as established by exacting research, was no great surprise. But that an unaberrated individual was vigorously repelled by evil and yet gained enormous strength was astonishing, since aberration had been so long incorrectly supposed to be the root of strength and ambition according to authorities since the time of Plato. That a man contained a mechanism which recorded with diabolical accuracy when the man was observably and by all presumable tests "unconscious" was newsworthy and surprising.

To the layman, the relationship of prenatal life to mental function has not entirely been disregarded, since for centuries beyond count people were concerned with "prenatal influence." To the psychiatrist, the psychologist and psychoanalyst, prenatal memory had long been an accepted fact since "memories of the womb" were agreed to influence the adult mind. But the prenatal aspect of the mind came as an entire surprise to Dianetics: an unwanted and, at the time, unwelcome observation. Despite existing beliefs—which are not scientific facts—that the fetus had memory, the psychiatrist and other workers believed, as well, that memory could not exist in a human being until myelin sheathing was formed around the nerves. This was as confusing to Dianetics as it was to psychiatry. After much work over some years, the exact influence prenatal life had on the later mind was established by Dianetics with accuracy.

There will be those who, uninformed, will say that Dianetics "accepts and believes in" prenatal memory. Completely aside from the fact that an exact science does not "believe," but establishes and proves facts, Dianetics emphatically does *not* believe in prenatal memory. Dianetics had to invade cytology and biology and form many conclusions by research; it had to locate and establish both the reactive mind and the hidden engram banks never before known before it came upon "prenatal" problems. It had been discovered that the engram recording was probably done on the cellular level, that the engram bank was contained in the cells. It was then discovered that the cells, reproducing from one generation to the next, within the organism, apparently carried with them their own memory banks. The cells are the first echelon of structure, the basic building blocks. They built the analytical mind. They operate, as the whip, the reactive mind. Where one has human cells, one has potential engrams. Human cells begin with the zygote, proceed in development with the embryo, become the fetus and finally the infant. Each stage of this growth is capable of reaction. Each stage in the growth of the colony of cells finds them fully cells, capable of recording engrams. In Dianetics, prenatal memory is not considered since the standard banks which will someday serve the completed analyzer in the infant, child and man are not themselves complete. There is neither "memory" nor "experience" before the nerves are sheathed as far as Dianetic therapy is concerned. But Dianetic therapy is concerned with *engrams,* not memories, with *recordings,* not experience. And wherever there are human cells, engrams are demonstrably possible and when physical pain was present, engrams can be demonstrated to have been created.

The engram is a recording like the ripples in the groove of a phonograph record: it is a complete recording of everything which occurred during the period of pain. Dianetics can locate, with its techniques, any engram which the cells have hidden, and in therapy the patient will often discover himself to be upon the prenatal cellular time track. There he will locate engrams and he goes there only because engrams exist there. Birth is an engram and is recovered by Dianetics *as a recording,* not as a *memory.* By return and the cellular extension of the time track, zygote pain storage can be, and is, recovered. It is *not* memory. It impinged upon the analytical mind and it obstructed the standard banks where memory is stored. This is a very great difference from prenatal memory. Dianetics recovers *prenatal engrams* and finds them responsible for much aberration and discovers that any longing for the womb is not present in any patient, but that engrams sometimes dictate a return to it, as in some regressive psychoses which then attempt to remake the body into a fetus.

This matter of prenatal life is discussed here at length in this synopsis to give the reader a perspective on the subject. We are dealing here with an exact science, precision axioms and new skills of application. By them we gain a command over aberration and psychosomatic ills. And with them we take an evolutionary step in the development of Man which places him yet another stage above his distant cousins of the animal kingdom.

A first edition of what readers of 1950 dubbed *The Book!*

DIANETICS

THE MODERN SCIENCE OF MENTAL HEALTH

A HANDBOOK OF

DIANETIC THERAPY

L. RON HUBBARD

Bay Head, New Jersey

Above A second-floor lounge allows visitors to walk Ron's greater philosophic path through historical artifacts and documentary presentations, replete with recollections from friends, students and colleagues

Right Also on display in the Bay Head lounge are representative editions of *Dianetics* in fifty languages and iconic imagery from a global movement those editions have inspired

Far right top The Living Room at Bay Head as it was when L. Ron Hubbard organized and coached the first Dianetics co-audit. All furnishings are historically authentic, even including the 1950 television and driftwood in the fireplace collected from the Bay Head beach.

Far right bottom Seated at this desk in a second-floor bedroom, L. Ron Hubbard authored *Dianetics: The Modern Science of Mental Health*. The typewriter is a Remington Noiseless (manual). The text ran 160,000 words, and it was completed between the first week of January and the 10th of February 1950.

Bay Head, New Jersey 45

The L. Ron Hubbard Heritage Site and birthplace of Dianetics: So it was in the winter of 1950, so it is today. Meticulously restored in every respect, visitors may now explore Ron's home along the waterfront of Bay Head, New Jersey, and find it exactly as he left it when presenting his new science of the mind with these immortal words: "Dianetics is an adventure. It is an exploration into *Terra Incognita,* the human mind, that vast and hitherto unknown realm half an inch back of our foreheads."

Bay Head, New Jersey

CHAPTER THREE

The Golden Dawn
OF SCIENTOLOGY

The Golden Dawn of Scientology

THE MATERIALS OF DIANETICS AND SCIENTOLOGY ARE contained in some ten thousand writings and three thousand tape-recorded lectures. In the main, those materials are concerned with the application of L. Ron Hubbard philosophic principles—the auditing processes toward greater awareness and ability, the assist processes

Left Phoenix, Arizona, 1952: Ron (seated on bench) with seminal circle of Scientology students

for the relief of physical illness and emotional distress, the means for resolving difficulties in the workplace, ethical failings, learning disabilities and, frankly, much, much more. Yet the philosophic root of Dianetics and Scientology, the core truth upon which all is based, could hardly be simpler:

"The spirit is the source of all. You are a spirit."

It is a unique statement and, factually, found nowhere else in the whole of philosophic, religious or scientific thought. To be sure, even in the most expansive Gnostic scriptures, one finds nothing as exalted as L. Ron Hubbard's statement on our spiritual essence. Nor does one find anything approaching the goal of Scientology—not to deliver a soul to the presence of God, but to recover one's own godlike compassion, wisdom and causality as an immortal, imperishable being.

Such was the central revelation of L. Ron Hubbard's research and discovery through early 1952 and such was the message he delivered to an unsuspecting world in 1954. Presented here are three landmark documents from those years.

Left Phoenix, Arizona, 1954

Above The L. Ron Hubbard "Desert Laboratory" below the Camelback Mountain in Phoenix, Arizona. It was here, through the fateful spring of 1952, Ron empirically demonstrated the human spirit can separate from and operate independently of the body: thus he arrived at the nexus of science and religion and thus the founding of Scientology.

The first is a *Journal of Scientology* article entitled "Man's Search for His Soul." It is pivotal in every respect. In point of fact, it is here L. Ron Hubbard writes of at last reaching "that merger point where science and religion meet" and thus a hallowed place where the human soul could no longer be ignored.

The second article presented here is entitled "Is It Possible to Be Happy?" It is a published transcription of an L. Ron Hubbard radio broadcast from December 1954. It is particularly notable for Ron's plain-spoken discussion of Scientology miracles and so bears upon a fascinating footnote of the day. It follows from the fact Phoenix was then predominantly fundamentalist and saw many an itinerant evangelist claiming to heal afflicted sinners sight unseen. In reply, a local Church of Christ offered a $1,000 reward for anyone providing incontrovertible proof of a miracle. In fact, however, the offer was a sham and actually intended to discredit out-of-town revivalist healers from encroaching on established ministries. The reward was also intended to reinforce orthodox dogma that only the Savior accomplished miracles. Hence, the chagrin when a Church of Scientology indeed delivered proof that the withered arm of a four-year-old boy

"miraculously" resumed normal growth patterns after but five hours of Scientology processing.

Also dating from 1954, we present "What Is Scientology?" It is one in a series of articles published under a "Golden Dawn" banner and originally intended for Phoenix at large. Accordingly, *The Golden Dawn* comprised an invitation to L. Ron Hubbard introductory lectures (initially convened at a newly founded Church of Scientology along East Roosevelt Street and latterly at the Monroe School auditorium). As such, here are truths from the pinnacle of Scientology presented in everyday fashion as an introduction to immortality.

Finally, and by way of background on all articles to follow, let us reiterate the intensity and depth of research through these days. To wit: L. Ron Hubbard was categorically the first to identify the capabilities of exterior beings and the first again to verify the fact of immortality. He was also the first to measure manifestations of energy from the life source itself. That is, and quite literally by means of oscilloscope, he registered wavelengths emitted directly from the human spirit.

So, yes, we are indeed entering rich country where science and religion finally meet. And, yes, it is a place where, at long last, is revealed the astonishing truth of human existence. ■

Scientology

Published by the Hubbard Association of Scientologists

Jan. 15, 1954   Issue 23-G

MAN'S SEARCH FOR HIS SOUL

by L. Ron Hubbard

For countless ages past, Man has been engaged upon a search.

All thinkers in all ages have contributed their opinion and considerations to it. No scientist, no philosopher, no leader has failed to comment upon it. Billions of men have died for one opinion or another on the subject of this search. And no civilization, mighty or poor, in ancient or in modern times, has endured without battle on its account.

The human soul, to the civilized and barbaric alike, has been an endless source of interest, attention, hate or adoration.

To say today that I have found the answer to all riddles of the soul would be inaccurate and presumptuous. To discount what I have come to know and to fail to make that known after observing its benefits would be a sin of omission against Man.

Today, after twenty-five years of inquiry and thought and after three years of public activity wherein I observed the material at work and its results, I can announce that in the knowledge I have developed, there must lie the answers to that riddle, to that enigma, to that problem—the human soul. For under my hands and others', I have seen the best in Man rehabilitated.

For the time since I first made a Theta Clear, I have been, with some reluctance, out beyond any realm of the scientific known. And now that I have myself cleared half a hundred, and auditors I have trained, many times that, I must face the fact that we have reached that merger point where science and religion meet, and we must now cease to pretend to deal with material goals alone.

We cannot deal in the realm of the human soul and ignore the fact. Man has too long pursued this search for its happy culmination here to be muffled by vague and scientific terms.

Religion, not science, has carried this search, th[rough] war, through the millennia. Science has all but sw[ept] lowed Man with an ideology which denies the sou[l, a] symptom of the failure of science in that search.

One cannot now play traitor to the men of God [who] sought these ages past to bring Man from the dark[ness.] We in Scientology belong in the ranks of the seeker[s] after truth, not in the rear guard of the makers [of the] atom bomb.

However, science too has had its role in the[se en]deavors. And nuclear physics, whatever crim[es] against Man, may yet be redeemed by having [given] aid in finding for Man the soul of which scien[ce has] but deprived him.

No auditor can easily close his eyes to the [results] achieves today or fail to see them superior. [For what] rialistic technologies he earlier used. For w[e know,] with all else we know, that the human sou[l is the] only effective therapeutic agent that we [have—and] goals, no matter our miracles with bodies [and] physical health and better men.

Scientology is the science of knowi[ng.] It has taught us that a man is his ow[n soul.] And it gives us little choice but to an[nounce that] no matter how it receives it, that n[ow science and] religion have joined hands and tha[t we can] perform those miracles for which [Man's] search has hoped.

The individual may hate God [or] cannot ignore, however, the evid[ence that he is his own] soul. Thus we have resolved ou[r problem of the] answer simple.

15 January 1954

MAN'S SEARCH FOR HIS SOUL

by L. Ron Hubbard

For countless ages past, Man has been engaged upon a search.

All thinkers in all ages have contributed their opinion and considerations to it. No scientist, no philosopher, no leader has failed to comment upon it. Billions of men have died for one opinion or another on the subject of this search. And no civilization, mighty or poor, in ancient or in modern times, has endured without battle on its account.

The human soul, to the civilized and barbaric alike, has been an endless source of interest, attention, hate or adoration.

To say today that I have found the answer to all riddles of the soul would be inaccurate and presumptuous. To discount what I have come to know and to fail to make that known after observing its benefits would be a sin of omission against Man.

Today, after twenty-five years of inquiry and thought and after three years of public activity wherein I observed the material at work and its results, I can announce that in the knowledge I have developed, there must lie the answers to that riddle, to that enigma, to that problem—the human soul. For under my hands and others', I have seen the best in Man rehabilitated.

For the time since I first made a *Theta Clear,* I have been, with some reluctance, out beyond any realm of the scientific known. And now that I have myself cleared half a hundred, and auditors I have trained, many times that, I must face the fact that we have reached that merger point where science and religion meet, and we must now cease to pretend to deal with material goals alone.

We cannot deal in the realm of the human soul and ignore the fact. Man has too long pursued this search for its happy culmination here to be muffled by vague and scientific terms.

Religion, not science, has carried this search, this war, through the millennia. Science has all but swallowed Man with an ideology which denies the soul, a symptom of the failure of science in that search.

One cannot now play traitor to the men of God who sought these ages past to bring Man from the darkness.

We in Scientology belong in the ranks of the seekers after truth, not in the rear guard of the makers of the atom bomb.

However, science too has had its role in these endeavors. And nuclear physics, whatever crime it does against Man, may yet be redeemed by having been of aid in finding for Man the soul of which science had all but deprived him.

No auditor can easily close his eyes to the results he achieves today or fail to see them superior to the materialistic technologies he earlier used. For we can know, with all else we know, that the human soul, freed, is the only effective therapeutic agent that we have. But our goals, no matter our miracles with bodies today, exceed physical health and better men.

Scientology is the science of knowing how to know. It has taught us that a man *is* his own immortal soul. And it gives us little choice but to announce to a world, no matter how it receives it, that nuclear physics and religion have joined hands and that we in Scientology perform those miracles for which Man through all his search has hoped.

The individual may hate God or despise priests. He cannot ignore, however, the evidence that he is his own soul. Thus we have resolved our riddle and found the answer simple.

IS IT POSSIBLE TO BE HAPPY?

by L. Ron Hubbard

Is it possible to be happy?

A great many people wonder whether or not happiness even exists in this modern, rushing world. Very often an individual can have a million dollars, he can have everything his heart apparently desires and is still unhappy. We take the case of somebody who has worked all his life. He's worked hard. He's raised a big family. He's looked forward to that time of his life when he, at last, could retire and be happy and be cheerful and have lots of time to do all the things he wanted to do. And then we see him after he's retired and is he happy? No. He's sitting there thinking about the good old days when he was working hard.

Our main problem in life is happiness.

The world today may or may not be designed to be a happy world. It may or may not be possible for you to be happy in this world. And yet, nearly all of us have the goal of being happy and cheerful about existence.

And then, very often, we look around at the world around us and say, "Well, nobody could be happy in this place." We look at the dirty dishes in the sink and the car needing a coat of paint and the fact that we need a new gas heater, we need a new coat, we need new shoes or we'd just like to have better shoes, and say, "Well, how could anybody *possibly* be happy when, actually, he can't have everything he wants? He's unable to do all the things he'd like to do and, therefore, this environment doesn't *permit* a person to be as happy as he could be."

Well, I'll tell you a funny thing. A lot of philosophers have said this many, many times, but the truth of the matter is that all the happiness you will ever find lies in *you*.

You remember when you were maybe five years old and you went out in the morning and you looked at the day—and it was a very, very beautiful day. You looked at flowers and they were

very beautiful flowers. Twenty-five years later, you get up in the morning, you take a look at the flowers—they are wilted. The day *isn't* a happy day. Well, what's changed? You know they are the same flowers, it's the same world. Something must have changed. Well, probably it was *you*.

Actually, a little child derives all of his pleasure in life from the grace he puts upon life. He waves a magic hand and turns all manner of interesting things into being out in the society. Where does he do this? He goes down and he looks at the cop. Here's this big, strong brute of a man riding this iron steed, up and down. Boy, he'd like to be a cop. Yes sir, he'd sure like to be a cop! Twenty-five years later, he looks at that cop riding up and down, checking his speedometer and says, "Doggone these cops!"

"A lot of philosophers have said this many, many times, but the truth of the matter is that all the happiness you will ever find lies in you."

Well, what's changed here? Has the cop changed? No. Just the *attitude* toward the cop. One's attitude toward life makes every possible difference in one's living. You know, you don't have to study a thousand ancient books to discover that fact. But sometimes it needs to be pointed out again that life doesn't change so much as *you*.

Once upon a time, perhaps, you were thinking of being married and having a nice home and having a nice family and everything would be just right. And the husband would come home, you see, and you'd put dinner on the table and everybody would be happy about the whole thing. And then you got married and it maybe didn't quite work out. Somehow or other, he comes home late, he's had an argument with the boss and he doesn't feel well. He doesn't want to go to the movies and he doesn't see how you have any work to do anyhow. After all, you just sit home all day and do nothing. And you know he doesn't do any work either. He disappears out of the house, he's gone and he comes back later in the evening and he hasn't done anything either. Quite an argument could ensue over this and, actually, both of you have worked quite hard.

Well, what do we do in a condition like this? Do we just break up the marriage? Or touch a match to the whole house? Or throw the kids in the garbage can and go home to Mama? Or what do we do?

Well, there are many, many, many things we could do and the least of them is to take a look at the environment. Just look around and say, "Where am I? What *am* I doing *here?*" And then, once you've found out where you were, why, try to find out how you could make that a little more habitable.

The day when you stop building your own environment, when you stop building your own surroundings, when you stop waving a magic hand and gracing everything around you with magic and beauty, things cease to be magical, things cease to be beautiful.

Well, maybe you've just neglected somewhere back in the last few years to wave that magic hand.

Other people seek happiness in various ways. They seek it hectically. It's as though it is some sort of a mechanism that exists. It's made up. Maybe it's a little machine, maybe it's something that's parked in a cupboard or maybe happiness is down at the next corner. Maybe it's someplace else. They are looking for *something*. Well, the odd part of it is, the only time they'll ever find something is when they put it there *first*. Now, this doesn't seem very creditable, but it is quite true.

Below
Another view of Ron's Phoenix home at the foot of Camelback Mountain and from where he would write of stones turning red in the first dawn's light

Those people who have become unhappy about life *are* unhappy about life solely and completely because life has ceased to be made by them. Here we have the single difference in a human being. We have that human being who is unhappy, miserable and isn't getting along in life, who is sick, who doesn't see brightness. Life is handling, running, changing, making *him*. Here we have somebody who is happy, who is cheerful, who is strong, who finds there is something worth doing in life. What do we discover in this person? We find out that he is making life. Now, there is actually the single difference: Are you making life or is life making you?

And when we go into this, we find out that a person has stopped making life because he himself has decided that life cannot be made. Some failure, some small failure—maybe not graduating with the same class, maybe that failure that had to do with not marrying quite the first man or woman who came along and seemed desirable, maybe the failure of having lost a car or just some minor thing in life started this attitude. A person looked around one day and said, "Well, I've lost." And after that, life makes him, he doesn't make life anymore.

Well, this would be a very dreadful situation if nothing could be done about it. But the fact of the matter is it's the easiest problem of all the problems Man faces: changing himself and changing the attitudes of those around him. It's very, very easy to change somebody else's attitude. Yet you are totally dependent upon other people's attitudes. Somebody's attitude toward you may make or break your life. Did it ever occur to you that your home holds together probably because of the attitude the other person has toward you? So there's two problems here. You have to change two attitudes: one, your attitude toward somebody else and, two, their attitude toward you.

Well, are there ways to do these things? Yes, fortunately, there are.

For many, many, many centuries, Man has desired to know how to change the mind and condition of himself and his fellows. Actually, Man hadn't accumulated enough information to do this up to relatively few years ago. But we're living in a very fast-paced world. We're living in a world where magic is liable to occur at any time, and has.

Man now understands a great many things about the universe he lives in which he never understood before. And amongst the things which he now understands is the human mind. The human mind is not an unsolved problem. Nineteenth-century psychology did not solve the problem. That doesn't mean that it hasn't been solved.

In modern times, the most interesting miracles are taking place all across this country and across the other continents of Earth. What do these miracles consist of? They consist of people becoming well. It consists of people who were unhappy becoming happy once more. It consists of abolishing the danger inherent in many of the illnesses and in many of the conditions of Man. And yet the answer has been with Man all the time. Man has been able to reach out and find this answer, but perhaps Man himself had to change. Perhaps he had to come up into modern times to find out that the physical universe was not composed of demons and ghosts, to outlive his superstitions, to outlive the ignorance of his forebears. Perhaps he had to do everything, including invent the atom bomb, before he could find himself.

"Those people who have become unhappy about life are unhappy about life solely and completely because life has ceased to be made by them."

Well, he has pretty well mastered the physical universe now. The physical universe is to him, now, rather a pawn—he can do many things with it. And, having conquered that, he can now conquer himself. The truth of the matter is he *has* conquered himself.

Scientology came about because of Man's increased knowledge of energy. Man became possessed of more information about energy than he had ever had before in all of his history. And amongst that, he came into possession of information about the energy which is his own mind.

The body *is* an energy mechanism. Naturally, a person who cannot handle energy could not handle a body. He would be tired, he would be upset, he would be unhappy. As he looks all around him, he finds nothing *but* energy.

If he knew a great deal about energy—particularly the energy of himself, the energy that made him think, the energy that *was* himself and the space which surrounded him—he, of course, would know himself. And that, in the final essence, has been his goal for many thousands of years: to know himself.

Scientology has made it possible for him to do so.

WHAT IS SCIENTOLOGY?

by L. RON HUBBARD

Man, for all the days of which we have record, has sought the answer to the riddle of himself.

In the ages past he has aspired to wisdom upon a thousand paths.

The earliest peoples, the Vedics, the Buddhists, the Taoists and the Christians have all yearned toward the knowingness which would open the doors of the Universe and discover more splendid states.

"Scientology" is a word in the tradition of all such words. It means in English the same as its counterparts in Hindu, in Sanskrit, in Hebrew and Latin. "Veda," "Tao," "Dhyana," and many other religious words mean exactly what "Scientology" means: the study of Wisdom.

Scientology embraces that knowingness necessary to the resolution of problems, such as those found in any human situation, whether the magnitude of the problem is personal or community in size.

Specifically, in Scientology we carry forward ten thousand years of known religious search into the mystery of life.

The efforts of Dharma, Lao-tzu, Gautama, Moses and Christ have given Man his principal lodestars upon this path.

The wisdom sought was the actuality of life, the identity of Creator of Life, and the actuality and identity of the human soul. The technology sought by all religious sages in all Man's past was the salvation of the human soul.

By fascinating adventures and through many difficulties this wisdom has come, factually, into the hands of modern man under the word which groups such wisdom and technology—"Scientology."

Scientology masters various body ills and solves problems of the mind, but this is natural that it would and such is a small use of it.

Scientology describes the human soul and frees it by simple technology.

A "Scientologist" is one who knows and practices Scientology on others. A Scientologist is an expert in human affairs. The long-trained Scientologist is an ordained minister. To be a Doctor of Divinity in Scientology one must have studied some thousands of hours or many times as long as doctors in comparable professions.

There are also "lay practitioners" in Scientology, as in many churches. These are sometimes trained for a few months and are entrusted with fairly routine matters.

There are Scientologists of many faiths and creeds. To be a Scientologist or to be interested in or use Scientology, it is not necessary to quit a church or faith. On the contrary, one should remain with and assist those of his denomination.

The Church of Scientology seeks no empire in this universe. It is a religious organization containing many creeds and faiths.

There are two categories of religion—the first is religious wisdom, the second is religious practice. The first is composed entirely of teachings; the second is composed of opinions and practices.

Various mutually used writings serve many faiths. So it is with Scientology.

The Church of Scientology operates on its own creed. It is completely independent of the Hubbard Association of Scientologists International.

Scientology is a wisdom of how to free and heal the human soul.

"Scientology is a wisdom of how to free and heal the human soul" —LRH

Phoenix, Arizona

Above The Camelback study where Ron distilled two decades of deeply probing inquiry into *Scientology 8-80*—a first definitive description of an all-knowing, all-embracive life source

Right The Janssen piano with which Ron conducted seminal research into the nature of pure aesthetics as an actual wavelength approximating emanations of the human spirit itself

Far right top Interior view of Ron's home below Camelback Mountain: it was here, through the spring of 1952, he effectively isolated the immortal essence that is the human spirit

Far right bottom The Phoenix Room, replete with photographs and artifacts from Ron's trail of discovery to the founding of Scientology. Among other items of note are the first seals and certificates of Scientology as well as a prototypic Scientology Cross.

Phoenix, Arizona

L. Ron Hubbard's Phoenix, Arizona, home is now another landmark site on his greater trail toward the Rediscovery of the Human Soul. As such, it affords another opportunity to walk his extraordinary path of exploration and revelation.

Phoenix, Arizona

CHAPTER FOUR

A Word on Rediscovering the
HUMAN SOUL

A Word on Rediscovering the Human Soul

I N YET ANOTHER OVERARCHING WORD ON HIS LARGER philosophic quest, L. Ron Hubbard writes of an epic odyssey "down many highways, through many byroads, into many back alleys of uncertainty." It was a journey, as he further tells us, through "tumultuous oceans of data" and across landscapes littered with the "lonely bones" of those who trekked before him but never returned to tell of what they saw—a voyage of almost unimaginable hardships and vast splendor. Albeit less poetic, the altogether more descriptive explanation of that journey is found in a retrospective piece entitled "The Rediscovery of the Human Soul."

Begun in 1955 but never completed, the manuscript effectively tells of all that preceded what appears in this publication. As a word of general background, let us add a few salient points: Although events recounted here mark the commencement of Mr. Hubbard's philosophic search, he had previously spent several years, as he elsewhere puts it, "poking an inquisitive mind" into related fields. Of special note were his early psychoanalytic studies with United States Naval Commander Joseph Cheesman Thompson—a man remembered as the first United States military officer to study under Sigmund Freud in Vienna and among the first to apply Freudian theory to ethnology. Also bearing mention was L. Ron Hubbard's early friendship with the deeply spiritual Blackfeet tribesmen in and around his home in Montana, and what amounted to folkloric studies with a locally famous medicine man, known as "Old Tom." The point: in both cases, and well before his arrival at George Washington University, the young Ron Hubbard had pondered much. Finally, and as referenced here, he had also spent nearly two years in a prerevolutionary China and, in fact, had been among the first Westerners after Marco Polo to gain entrance into forbidden Tibetan lamaseries scattered through the southern hills of Manchuria.

Washington, DC, 1962: *"For better or worse, I concluded that Man had better know not just a little more about dying but a lot more about Man. And that shaped my destiny." —LRH*

The Founding Church of Scientology, Washington, DC, 1957

Specifically regarding "The Rediscovery of the Human Soul," let us add that in referencing the "formidable and slightly mad" chief of George Washington University's psychology department, he is actually speaking of Dr. Fred August Moss, infamous among students for cunningly trick questions and running rats through gruesome electrical mazes. Meanwhile the "very famous psychiatrist" who reviews Ron's calculations on human memory capacity was none other than William Alanson White, then superintendent of Washington, DC's St. Elizabeths Hospital and still celebrated for his outspoken opposition to psychosurgery. Most importantly, however, let us simply understand this: In recalling his work through these years, and particularly his efforts to isolate the repository of human memory, the young Ron Hubbard was factually raising a crucial philosophic question. That is, when we attempt to explain all human memory in terms of purely physical phenomena, we will ultimately find ourselves staring at the singular flaw in the whole of the Western scientific creed. Namely, no diagram of the human brain can account for all we are capable of remembering (much less imagining). It was not for nothing, then, that William Alanson White remarked, in response to Ron's memory calculations, "You have just laid to waste the entire foundation of psychiatric and neurological theory."

Today, of course, psychologists, psychiatrists, neurologists, et al., continue to turn themselves inside out in an effort to propose theories broad enough to explain human memory in purely physical terms. (One of the latest involves a model of *scattered* memory traces along synaptic contacts so that memories are superimposed upon one another. Another holds that memory is re-created through dynamic neural interplay.) But in either case, questions Ron posed in 1932 are still not answerable within a wholly material context. Hence, the increasingly frequent admissions from the scientific community that perhaps, after all, as L. Ron Hubbard later phrased it, "Man, as a learned whole, knew damned little about the subject." ∎

The Rediscovery of the Human Soul

THE REDISCOVERY OF THE HUMAN SOUL

by L. RON HUBBARD

ONCE UPON A TIME Man knew he had a soul. He would have been shocked if he had been told that someday a book would have to be written to inform him, as a scientific discovery, that he had one.

And yet that is what this is about. It is not about *your* soul. It is not designed to tell you to be good or bad or a Christian or a Yogi. It is written to tell you the story of the rediscovery of the human soul as a scientific, demonstrable fact.

Here, at a moment when all religions everywhere face extinction by communism, psychiatry, psychology, dialectic materialism and other -ologies and -isms without number, one might believe this was an effort to create adequate religious fervor to stem the onslaught of the propaganda pamphlets which, all other things aside, are really the most hideous aspect of these threats to Man. However, this volume seeks no such thing. It is doubtful if religious control of Man was very successful, either. In the scorch of friction created by such conflicts, one might not realize that the soul is worth investigating and writing about for its own sake, not for the sake of capital to be gained from its establishment or extinction.

The tale of the rediscovery of the soul is a considerable adventure entirely from the philosophic and experimental aspect. The adventure has been quite heightened by the amount of preconception and rebuff encountered because of these -isms and -ologies. One would think that ideologies were quite swollen with their fine opinion of themselves to believe that any investigation of the soul would, of course, be meant as a personal affront to each or all of them. One conceives the view, after he has been awhile investigating the soul, that among all these modern disagreements there existed only one agreement: that the subject of the human soul, for bad or good, was only within the personal sphere of each. Thus, publishing this will in itself be an adventure, for it will discover among these -isms and -ologies, each one, the conceit that it itself is being attacked. And to "attack" that many oppositions at one fell charge requires in an author either the hide of a rhinoceros, the Citadel of a Christophe, or the legs of an impala. Having none of these, but only a certain confidence in the stupidity of all these schools of slavery, we locate in ourselves a willingness to accept the risk if not the combat.

> *"Once upon a time Man knew he had a soul. He would have been shocked if he had been told that someday a book would have to be written to inform him, as a scientific discovery, that he had one."*

Our main controversy, quite aside from minor ones, is whether or not the soul or knowledge about it could be considered a "scientific subject." For by definition in these dialectic times, science is a somethingness which considers itself concerned entirely with matters of matter and has sought to accumulate to itself alone—much like other -isms and -ologies—the entire proprietorship of knowledge, and has then sought to demonstrate that knowledge is only to be found in materialism. This somewhat detoured view becomes artificial on its first inspection. *Science* means only "truth," being derived from the Greek word *scio*, which is "knowing in the fullest sense of the word." More severely and lately used, "science" infers an organization of knowledge. And if this is the case, then this material concerning the human soul, being based on critically observational knowledge and being organized, certainly meets the criteria of "scientific" knowledge.

Being, then, based on observable, mensurable truth or knowledge and being organized, we assigned to this body of information about the human soul the word *Scientology,* which is to say, the "knowledge of knowledge" or "knowing how to know" or "study of truth," thus and thereby, with the word, taking sides with the "-ologies." But we could just as well call this material "soulism" or "the doctrine of the human soul" and take the alignments of the "-isms," thus, so to speak, edging over on the good side of each and thus avoiding war.

Scientology, as a word, is quite necessary, since we need an identifying symbol to represent these particular discoveries and data and the methodology of their use and to prevent our making errors in conversation. The subject of the soul lends itself readily to any branch of any knowledge and to keep oriented and localized with the information contained herein, we need the word.

Very well. Now that we have, we hope, announced our political climate, or lack of one, and have given a word to what we are doing, let us examine *what* we are doing.

We are studying the soul or spirit. We are studying it as itself. We are not trying to use this study to enhance some other study or belief. And we are telling the story of how it came about that the soul needed rediscovering. And now that we've rediscovered it, we are also discovering if the information thus attained can in any way assist us to live better or, for that matter, die better.

Thus, you can plainly see that this is perfectly safe to read. It does not seek to alter your ideological or religious beliefs. If these alter simply because you read this, no one is to blame but yourself and it was not the author's intention to tamper.

Of course, if you *do* read this, your ideological and religious beliefs will alter—there's no doubt of that. However, remember, should the idea of blaming anyone occur to you, that whatever actually *happens,* we didn't really *intend* to change your philosophic pattern. All we intended to do, quite innocently, was to give you some data about the human soul. Not even your own soul, just the soul in general.

Well, you've been warned.

The story starts in the Physics Laboratories of George Washington University in 1930. Quite coincidentally, at almost this same time, Professor Brown, in charge of that department, was launching experiments which within fifteen years would bring forth an atomic bomb upon Earth, largely through Dr. George Gamow, an assistant in this same laboratory.

Unwitting of the ferocity being planned within a few yards of me, I was engaged upon an experiment about poetry. Now, usually poetry has little to do with a physics lab, but this time it did. Majoring in engineering a trifle under duress and studying nuclear physics with a skeptical eye, my tedium had found a relief in conceiving that one might find why poetry in any language sounded like poetry, whether one spoke the language or not.

Using an aged Koenig photometer to measure voice vibrations, I was reading a line of Browning and then a line of prose, alternately, and studying any difference between the symmetry of vibrations in the poetry as contrasted to the prose. I discovered after a little that there was a definite symmetry and was about to concoct a more complex test when it struck me that the mind was *not* a Koenig photometer. I drew back and looked studiously at the ugly machine, with its four mirrors and glass frame, and commented to myself that it would be a frighteningly uncomfortable thing to have kicking about between one's ears. *But* if one did not have one between one's ears, one *did,* or at least *must,* have some kind of mechanism which would translate and measure not only the impulse of sound but also the symmetry of that sound. And, having measured it, that something did the additional trick not only of storing that symmetry but of recalling and viewing it at will.

Below
Koenig photometer, the instrument with which Ron conducted early experiments on the universality of poetic rhythm

The Rediscovery of the Human Soul 81

Thus was born a search, a search which went on for a quarter of a century. Thus was born the train of intuition, observation and experiment which finally rediscovered, as a scientific fact, the soul, and gained methods of doing things to it, for it and with it with scientific certainty.

But here in 1930, serving out my time in "the salt mines of F Street," no such serious end was in real view. My interest, I must confess, went more to soaring planes at Congressional Airport, upsetting the faculty by my articles in the University paper and always making sure that the most demanded girl on the campus was the sweetheart of the professional engineering fraternity (and mine to dance with, of course).

Probably nothing would have come of my search at all if I had not tried to solve something of the problem by calling on the formidable and slightly mad chief of the psychology department. He, in the secrecy of his opinions of his fellows, mainly wanted to know what I was doing out of the engineering school and why I didn't leave such things properly to psychologists. This challenged me a

trifle. As a sensitive youth, spoiled by the courtesy of the Orient in which I had spent much precollege time, I objected to people being so thoroughly Occidental. And after I had laughed at him a few columns in the University paper, I wheedled all the psychology textbooks out of a psychology major (whose themes in English class I used to write) and heavied my eyelids, but not my understanding, by studying them hard during my German and Surveying lectures (which bored me intensely anyway). But though I studied and comprehended what I read, the comprehension, I began to believe, was a trifle one-sided. These texts, like the courtesy of the psychology dean, were somewhat wanting.

Like the picture of the picture of the picture on the cereal box, psychology simply assigned all this first to the brain and then to the cell. Going no further, it still failed to describe any sound-recording-recalling devices. With youthful scorn, I consigned psychology to that moldy heap of pretenses which so often pass their polysyllabic nonsense off as learning, and decided to think some more about thinking—a trick to say the least.

About this time, a biology major and I were accustomed to meeting after classes at (O bygone days) a speak-easy up 21st Street, for a round of blackjack and a couple shots after classes. And while trying to detour my eyes from his nimble fingers, he regaled me with bits and things about what went on in the world of biology. One day, he actually did manage to slip me the card I didn't want by remarking to me that the brain contained an exorbitant number of molecules of protein and that each molecule "had been discovered" to have holes in it. Fascinated, I bled him of data and a few days later made the time to calculate memory.

It seemed to me that if molecules had holes in them to a certain number, then memory, perchance, might be stored in these holes in the molecules. At least it was more reasonable than the texts I had read. But the calculation, done with considerably higher math than psychologists or biologists use, yet yielded a blank result. I calculated that memory was "made" at a certain rate and was stored in the holes in these punched protein molecules in the form of the most minute energy of which we had any record in physics. But despite the enormous number of molecular holes and the adequate amount of memory, the entire project yielded only this result: I was forced to conclude, no matter how liberal I became, that even with this system, certainly below cellular level, the brain did not have enough storage for more than three months of memory. And in that I could recall things quite vividly at least before the beginning of the semester, I was persuaded that either the mind could not remember anything or that much smaller energy particles existed than we knew about in nuclear physics.

Amusing, a decade later this theory, which I had imparted to a very famous psychiatrist complete with the figures, came back as an Austrian "discovery" and was widely accepted as the truth. I always wondered at the psychiatrist's carelessness in losing that last page, which declared by the same calculations that the mind could not remember.

Laying it all aside for a long time, I was yet recalled to my calculations by physics itself. There are some odd movements noticeable in atomic and molecular phenomena which aren't entirely accounted for. And supposing that a "smaller" energy might make these movements among the larger particles, I came face to face with the grossness of the measuring equipment with which we have always worked in physics. We have only streams of electrons, even today, to "see small." And I was so struck with the enormity of the terra incognita which physics had yet to invade that it seemed far simpler to do what I eventually did—went off and became a science fiction writer.

Living the rather romantic life of an author in New York, Hollywood and the Northwest, going abroad into savage cultures on expeditions to relax, I did little about my search until 1938, when a rather horrible experience took my mind closer to home than was my usual mental circuit. During an operation, I died under the anesthetic.

Brought back to unwillingly lived life by a fast shot of Adrenalin into the heart, I rather frightened my rescuers by sitting up and saying, "I know something if I could just think of it."

In my woods cabin in the Northwest, I had quite a little while to think of it. The experience had made me ill enough to keep me in a reading frame of mind and I didn't get far from a teapot, a blanket and books for some weeks.

The alarm caused those "nearest to me," when I sought to regale them with this adventure of death, amused me. That they were not disturbed that I had actually and utterly died medically and coroneresquely, they were dismayed that I would talk about it. Deciding it was not a popular subject, I nevertheless looked into the rather extensive library I sported and found that the thing was not unknown in human experience and that a chap named Pelley had even founded a considerable religious study on it. Quite plausibly, he went to Heaven and came back and lived to tell of it.

The psychiatric texts which I kept around, for unpronounceable ailments to put in the mouths of my fictional doctors, were as thoroughly alarmed as my near of kin. They called any such experiences by a nice ugly name, "delusion," and made fat paragraphs out of its mental unhealthiness. Only in that matter of unhealthiness could I agree with them. I always have, always will and did then consider that dying was unhealthy. They also seemed to feel that people who died ought to stay dead. Concluding that the littleness they knew about such happenings was best expressed by the voluminous inconclusions they wrote about it, I turned to the classic philosophers. And while these had much to say, very little of it was concisely to the point.

I realized, after wandering through some five hundred pounds of texts, some things which altered my life quite a bit more than merely dying. During those weeks in the cabin, my studies pressed me toward some conclusions. I concluded, first, that dying had not been very damaging. I concluded, second, that Man, as a learned whole, knew damned little about the subject. For better or worse, I concluded that Man had better know not just a little more about dying but a lot more about Man.

And that shaped my destiny.

L. RON HUBBARD DISCUSSES THE DEVELOPMENT OF HIS PHILOSOPHY

In November 1958, at the request of Dr. Stillson Judah, Professor of Religious History, Ron discussed both the philosophic background and working principles of Dianetics and Scientology. Although some of what is talked of here—Ron's examination of poetry, for example—has been touched upon earlier, the perspective is unique; for with Dr. Stillson Judah we have a man much intrigued with ideas, and it is the grand progression of L. Ron Hubbard's thinking he seeks through the course of this conversation.

Also keenly relevant here are Ron's statements on what followed from work at Oak Knoll, including the publication of Dianetics: The Modern Science of Mental Health *and, thereafter, his recognition of "what was looking at the pictures."*

Dr. Judah: *Where did the subject of Dianetics and Scientology start?*
LRH: The whole subject was actually born out of engineering. Both of these subjects stemmed from engineering, which was taken on top of five years of my study in the Orient as a boy.

From the age of about sixteen to about twenty-one, I spent a great deal of my time in the Orient and I was well acquainted with various Oriental schools. I came back and studied physical sciences and religion, which gave me a background of mathematics and physics. These taught me how to think, I hope, in a fairly disciplined fashion.

My basic interest was the field of religion. Buddhism, Taoism—these things were fascinating to me. However, I didn't think that they were very good for people. They couldn't possibly contain all of the answers, for this one

Dr. Stillson Judah

"Therefore we find ourselves in the middle of a moral and ethical science which applies to nothing more nor less than the human spirit" —LRH, Washington, DC, 1958

reason: the people who were practicing them were poor, unhealthy and in very, very bad relationship with the physical universe.

So quite by accident almost, in 1932, I was working in a George Washington University laboratory, trying to add up poetry. I couldn't understand why poetry, read in Japanese, would obviously be poetry to somebody who spoke only English, why poetry of various kinds was poetry even when translated. What was this thing called poetry? Interesting study, just in itself.

"In 1938 nobody—neither Darwin nor anyone else in the field of evolution—had stated a Basic Principle of Existence."

I picked up a Koenig photometer, one of these little gas photometers that you hold against the diaphragm while talking and it gives vocal vibrations. I made graphs of poetry. I wanted to know how the mind responded to those sounds, *why* the mind responded to those sounds. And it was a rather interesting study. I could not get any real basis for why the mind responded to certain sounds and rhythms and not to others. Why did the mind differentiate between noise and a note, for instance? This didn't seem to be a covered subject in my field.

I became interested enough to go to a George Washington University psychology laboratory, at that time run by Dr. Fred Moss. He floored me. Up to that time I had known Dr. Thompson, who was the first psychoanalyst of the US Navy. He was my bosom friend when I was a little boy. I, to a large degree, followed in his footsteps. He was very interested in psychotherapy, but I didn't pay him too much attention. I listened. And up to this interview with Dr. Moss, I hadn't known something: I hadn't known we didn't know.

It was a very odd thing for anybody educated in the engineering sciences—where you know what you know when you know it and how you know it—to be given a bunch of statements which didn't explain at all my problem. I was simply an engineer taking, on confidence, the fact that all other sciences, even those in human relations, were all well understood. And I ran into somebody who could not answer my questions. I read all of the books I could find in the Library of Congress on psychology and the mind. I found out I was looking at a field that didn't know what it knew. It didn't know. And it was a baffling thing to me.

I turned to philosophies of various kinds, still studying engineering. But I made this a very positive hunt. It wasn't until 1938 that I was totally convinced we didn't know, that we didn't have a Basic Principle of Existence, that there was no point of jump-off for the human mind, for the study of the human spirit. We didn't even know what a spirit was. We didn't have a definition for it. We said where it went and what would happen to it and how it could be punished, but we never said what it was. What was its relationship?

These questions could be answered very easily. I don't mean to get oratorical with you in any way, but these questions could have been answered perhaps in some field somewhere at some time, but I just couldn't seem to find the answers. Whether it was Nietzsche or Schopenhauer or Kant or any of the rest of them, these men were all groping.

So I said consistently to myself, "Here's a wide-open field."

Between my leaving the university and 1938 we were in a—.

Dr. Judah: *What university was that?*
LRH: George Washington.
Dr. Judah: *George Washington.*
LRH: We were in a depression, if you remember. Any job that I'd had offered me was long gone by the time I stepped out. I used my engineering in the field of writing—science fiction and so on. I spent a whole career before World War II as a successful writer. I was in Hollywood. I went on three expeditions to study wild and savage peoples and find out what they thought about things. And I paid for them with writing. I did very well as a writer. I was president of the American Fiction Guild. But all this time, all I was really doing was trying to eat and pay my way and pay for my research and finally get up to some point where I had some clue as to this Basic Principle of Existence.

In 1938 nobody—neither Darwin nor anyone else in the field of evolution—had stated a Basic Principle of Existence. And I said, "Then for good or bad, I'm going to have to state one in order to launch any sort of a further investigation." Because all I'd done was look at question marks.

And I did. The basic work that I wrote has never been published. I wrote a 125,000-word work and it has never seen the light of day.

Dr. Judah: *Why was that?*
LRH: I considered it much too inaccurate. It was a soar into the blue, merely an attempt to explain. It was an attempt to organize knowledge on the basis of a Dynamic Principle of Existence, to see if it could be done, see if it gave us answers in the field of the spirit. I didn't think of improving anybody or explaining religion or anything else. Just speculative work. Of course, it's never been released; it's full of errors and speculations and it's one more thing that issued from the ivory tower of philosophy and got nowhere.

It did bring me to an understanding, on an evaluation basis, of the Dynamic Principle of Existence of Survive, or Survival. I tried to evaluate along this line very heavily to see where we got. Because the one common denominator I could find in all races, types and activities was survival. Everybody seemed to be trying for survival. And when they no longer tried for survival, then they tried for its opposite: succumb. And these two things seemed to go together as the motivating principles of life.

War came along. Because I knew Asia, I was thrown into naval intelligence, commissioned. Early in the war, they returned nearly everybody who had been involved in it home and they wouldn't send them out there anymore. So they gave me command of a corvette and I finished up the war as a line officer, oddly enough.

Tremendously interesting things occurred during this period. For instance, I had enormous subjects for study, tremendous subjects for study, all this time. I had one crew that was 100 percent criminals. They were all criminals. They'd just taken them right straight out of Portsmouth and issued them to this corvette. A hundred men.

I spent the last year of my naval career in a naval hospital. Not very ill, but I had a couple of holes in me and they wouldn't heal. So they just kept me. And everywhere I looked there, I seemed to find men who were in difficulty, men who couldn't rationalize why they were there; they didn't know what they were doing. And I said, "Well, maybe the answer lies in the glandular system. Maybe this is a material answer after all." I spent most of that year down in the medical library studying the endocrine system, trying to find out if it got anywhere. Every answer led back to the fact that Man was motivated by something I had not yet put my finger on.

To make a long story short, after the war I returned to writing, but mostly to Dianetics and its preparation. And I found out what was entangling Man. He was tangling himself up with combinations of mental image pictures. And if you could do something to the pictures, you could do something to the man. Quite interesting. I entered now in a safe, sound field, where I was concerned. There was an energy, you could measure these pictures, they weren't imaginary. I found out they were measurable and did measure them. We were in a sound field of engineering. A very sound field, very satisfactory: you had your hands on some mass and you could produce a positive effect and things were traceable.

Unfortunately I was persuaded by Hermitage House to write a popular book on the subject. That book, *Dianetics: The Modern Science of Mental Health,* sold and sold and sold and it rode the top of the bestseller list. The only trouble is the editor made me guilty of exaggerations. Why this man did this I don't know. It did make his company a lot of money, but it brought me a lot of embarrassment. And the embarrassment was this: I had no organization, I had no finance, I had nothing. And all of a sudden the world was pounding on my door.

Dr. Judah: *This was the new mousetrap.*

LRH: Oh, it was the new mousetrap, that's for sure. College students came from every part of this country, people from all over the world. They presented cases I had never seen before. They presented greater difficulties than I had ever seen before. I didn't know what to do with many of these people. And I knew my study was a long way from an end.

I didn't have anything to do with the early Foundations. I was an advisor or something of the sort. My name was put on the board on an honorary basis more than anything else. I had a lot of people around who wanted to make a great deal of money. I couldn't see this at all. I wanted to get the answers to this and get, if anything, my reputation fished out of the ragbag and get this story written just a little further.

In the fall of 1951 I found out what was looking at the pictures. We had mental image pictures and up to that time we'd been studying them and their behavior, which is the reaction, stimulus-response mechanisms that psychology itself had been familiar with but never anatomized. I found out what was looking at the pictures and described it and found out that you could do things with it from a very practical standpoint that nobody had ever done before and found myself suddenly in the field of religion. Whether I wanted to be or not, there I was. Very simple: *the human soul was the fellow.*

This rather upset things because most religions speak to men about "You've got to take care of your soul." This wasn't the case, according to my findings. The fellow I was talking to *was* a soul. The only reason I knew these things were valuable was because I already knew Buddhism. I knew how many years a Buddhist could sit and meditate and how long a Lama priest could work to get a detached view of things. And I found out that, on some 50 percent of the people I ran into, I could attain this detached view of things in a matter of minutes. So I knew I wasn't looking at a weird phenomenon nor a psychotic manifestation. Psychiatry had known something about this, but they merely said it was a sure sign of craziness.

But the man was his own spirit and, whether I liked it or not, I was in the middle of a religion. The first organization I founded in this particular field was in 1952 in Phoenix, Arizona. It was called the Hubbard Association of Scientologists, composed of people who had become very interested in this work and wanted to see me get the show on the road.

I went on from there, working to find out what was the behavior of this thing called the human spirit. And I felt to some degree I'd arrived. At first I didn't even know that it wasn't a mass factor. Don't think I didn't have to turn myself around and upside down, because I had accustomed myself to thinking in totally scientific, totally realistic, lines. When I was dealing with something I couldn't sense, measure or experience but which was there, I certainly was going to sense, measure and experience to know the reason why. And I did, as a matter of fact. In London, in 1953, I built a meter which measures the responses of this thing while exteriorized from a being.

> *"I found out that you could improve the goodness of a man by improving the man. And he was more or less basically good."*

I finally satisfied myself that I was really looking at the thing that looked at the pictures, the thing that experienced the pictures, the thing that motivated the pictures and realized that unless we improved a man spiritually, all we could do was change his habit patterns. We wouldn't change his desire to do better. Maybe we could punish him into it or something, but unless we got a new view on the part of the individual and a new capability to handle his environment and himself, then we had a bad man or a deteriorating man. I found out that you could improve the goodness of a man by improving the man. And he was more or less basically good. This was a very great stroke of luck, as far as I was concerned. When you freed a man and separated him from past punishment, you found that he was good. That was a rather fabulous thing. Therefore we find ourselves in the middle of a moral and ethical science which applies to nothing more nor less than the human spirit.

Washington, DC

Above The L. Ron Hubbard Office at the Founding Church in Washington, DC: likewise restored to stand as it was when Ron helmed a then burgeoning Scientology movement across four continents

Right Reception at 1812 19th Street, now presenting a retrospective look at Ron's life in the nation's capital, very much including his inquiring trail at George Washington University, where he precipitously fell off the cliff of known knowledge

Far right top The Washington, DC, Lecture Hall and Chapel: site of historic LRH talks on decisive discoveries along the developmental path of Scientology. It was also here Ron performed the first Scientology religious services.

Far right bottom Reproduction line for LRH lectures: it was from this bank of Ampex recorders and copiers that L. Ron Hubbard taped lectures were originally duplicated for worldwide distribution

Washington, DC 93

The original Founding Church of Scientology, Washington, DC, at 1812 19th Street, now impeccably restored in every respect

CHAPTER FIVE

The
DEMYSTIFICATION
OF DEATH

The Demystification of Death

WHEN DISCUSSING THE PHENOMENA OF DEATH, ONE IS probably touching upon the single most universally pondered philosophic question. Moreover, and particularly what with a doubling of an American population beyond the age of sixty-five, one is discussing a matter of truly grave concern.

By way of introduction, let us briefly return to early 1952, when on the heels of Dianetics L. Ron Hubbard declared: "The further one investigated, the more one came to understand that here, in this creature Homo sapiens, were entirely too many unknowns." In particular, he cited "strange yearnings" for faraway lands, curious memories of distant times, and those with no observable training, suddenly, and quite inexplicably, speaking foreign tongues. Then, too, and herein lay the crux, there were cases soon on record, dozens actually, wherein those receiving Dianetics had not shown expected improvement until traumatic experience from what appeared to have been several lifetimes had been alleviated.

To appreciate what was unfolding, let us understand that if Dianetics involves "the tracing of experience" to discharge buried trauma, then it was found to be incumbent upon the Dianetics auditor to address the whole of that experience—even including, as Ron explained, "phenomena for which we have no adequate explanation." His first recorded statement on the matter was equally indeterminate. In reference to a case wherein remarkably convincing details of an apparently former death were offered, he very simply remarked, "We've got to keep an open mind about these things" and would not further commit himself. Privately, however, he seems to have remained unconvinced, and reasonably suggested the so-called former life sequence to be imaginative, perhaps representing a means of "taking refuge in a fictitious past." But in either case, and to this

London, England, 1955

he held firm, the matter clearly warranted further investigation.

To grasp what next ensued requires a short explanation of circumstances. Not long after the publication of *Dianetics: The Modern Science of Mental Health,* and in the wake of unprecedented popularity (the book soon topped bestseller lists, generated banner headlines and finally inspired nothing short of a national movement), the first Dianetic Research Foundation had formed in Elizabeth, New Jersey. Although nominally listed among the directors, Ron confined himself to further research, lectures and the training of students. The actual administration of Foundation affairs fell to others, and within that arrangement, he found himself facing a board resolution to prohibit any and all further discussion of past lives.

If one is to be entirely fair, those behind that now infamous New Jersey board resolution must not be accused of an arbitrary prejudice. After all, and particularly within mid-twentieth-century Western society, the notion of a former existence was nothing if not foreign. Moreover, when speaking of those from the New Jersey board, including Michigan physician Dr. Joseph Winter, former Western Electric engineer Donald Rogers and *Astounding Science Fiction* editor John W. Campbell, Jr.,

> "The further one investigated, the more one came to understand that here, in this creature Homo sapiens, were entirely too many unknowns."

one is speaking of quite a materially minded crew. Campbell, for example, had previously struggled with several elaborate theories to explain human thought in purely cellular terms and was otherwise much concerned that Dianetics remain on an acceptably scientific, i.e., material, footing. Meanwhile, the just as politically concerned Winter, in his capacity as Foundation medical director, continued to argue that Dianetics would never gain true acceptance (and all-important federal funding) unless amalgamated into the American psychological and psychiatric establishment.... Which, in turn, demanded nothing shake a psychological/psychiatric creed that defined our lives as a purely biochemical process beginning with our birth and ending with our death.

Much more might be said, including the fact that, quite in addition to a psychological/psychiatric aversion to evidence of past lives,

The first Scientology center for the British Commonwealth, otherwise known as the Hubbard Communications Office of London, circa 1960

a good part of Christian dogma stood opposed to the notion. The thinking is complex and quite deeply rooted in a Christian orthodoxy wherein the central appeal was a hope of *physical* resurrection. In brief, however, the argument is this: If, as suggested in various Gnostic scriptures, the human soul was destined to rebirth, then obviously the threat of eternal damnation tended to lose its sting. Which was not to say the sinner did not suffer under Gnostic doctrine. On the contrary, Earth itself became the unending Hell for those who lived, lifetime after lifetime, beyond the grace of God. Yet from a strictly ecumenical standpoint, a doctrine of reincarnation tended to undermine Church authority as the sole means of salvation and everlasting life through the grace of Christ. Moreover, it tended to undermine key sources of Church revenue, very much including the sale of indulgences. Consequently came the formal expunging of all such doctrine with the Second Synod of Constantinople in 553 A.D.

None of this, of course, figured into Ron's thinking. Rather, his concerns remained purely practical and solely determined by workability. Did those receiving auditing benefit from addressing what was perceived as traumatic experience from a former life or did

The Demystification of Death 101

they not? No other factor, whether political or philosophical, was deemed relevant. Besides which—and this in unqualified terms to members of the Foundation board—"You can't pass resolutions to say what is or isn't in the human mind."

Reprinted in the following pages is Ron's introductory note to what may be viewed as the culmination of such research, the 1960 *Have You Lived Before This Life?* The text is comprised of some forty cases wherein advanced Scientology auditing procedures were employed to alleviate difficulties stemming from former lives. What those cases tell us in a larger philosophic context is, of course, monumental and bears upon the whole of our existence...including the startling proposition, as LRH so bluntly puts it, "What we create in our societies during this lifetime affects us during our next lifetime." Equally startling were the results of those Scientology auditing procedures. There are more than a few documented cases, for example, wherein hopelessly crippled polio victims were restored to full mobility after—*only* after—addressing former lives. Finally, for those intrigued by such details, there was the subsequent case of a young Scientologist who recalled not only the circumstances of her former life, but the actual place of her burial. Whereupon she made her way to a southern English churchyard and there, just as recalled through the course of her auditing, stood the otherwise forgotten gravestone bearing her former name. ∎

> *"What we create in our societies during this lifetime affects us during our next lifetime."*

First edition of *Have You Lived Before This Life?* Comprising a compendium of cases recounting former life experience, this was the work that riveted readers with a startling proposition of immortality.

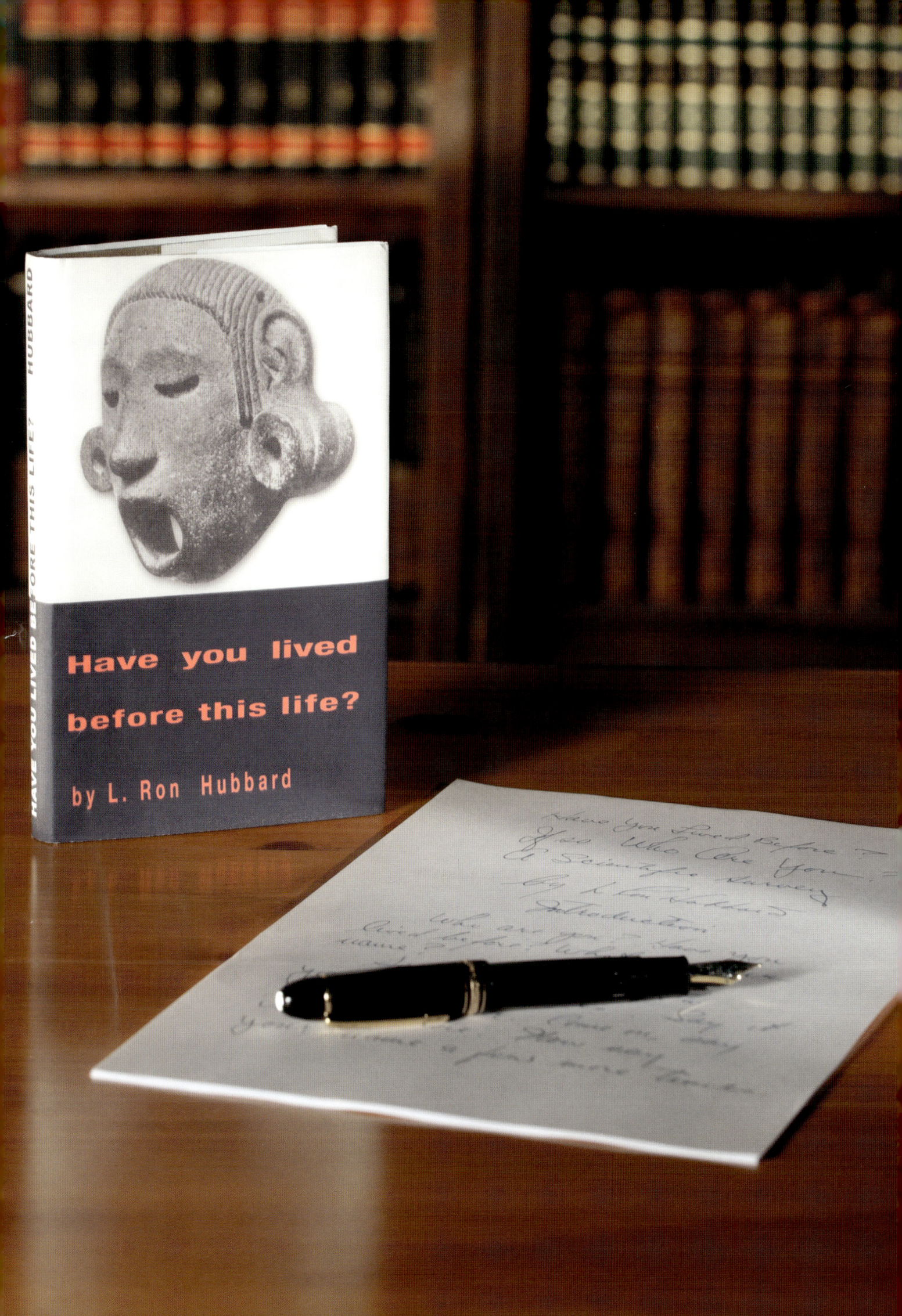

November 1958

A NOTE ON PAST LIVES

by L. Ron Hubbard

PAST LIVES, OR TIMES we have lived before, are suppressed by the painfulness of the memory. The memory is contained in mental image pictures which, on close viewing, are capable of developing a reality "more real" than present time.

Where a person has been tortured or killed without adequate reason, the injustice of it causes him or her to protest by holding in suspension in time the picture.

To restore memory on one's whole existence, it is necessary to bring one up to being able to confront such experiences.

A person with amnesia is looked upon as ill. What of a person who can remember only this life? Is this, then, not a case of amnesia on a grand scale?

Psychosomatic illness such as arthritis, asthma, rheumatism, heart trouble and on and on for a total of 70 percent of man's ills—and women's too—are the reaction of the body against a painful mental image picture, or *engram*. When this picture is cleared away—if it is the right picture—the illness usually abates.

The Scientologist can turn on actual fevers and turn them off just by restimulating mental image pictures in a person.

The recovery of whole memory could be said to be a goal of processing.

Past lives are "incredible" only to those who dare not confront them. In others, the fact of former existence can be quickly established subjectively.

There are many interesting cases on record since Dianetics gave impetus to Bridey Murphy. One was a case of a young girl, about five, who, hanging back at church, confided to her clergyman that she was worried about her "husband and children." It seems she had not forgotten them after "dying out of" another life five years before.

The clergyman did not at once send for the chaps in white coats. Instead he questioned the truly worried child closely.

She told him she had lived in a nearby village and what her name had been. She said where her former body was buried, gave him the address of her husband and children and what all their names were, and asked him to drive over and find out if they were all right.

The clergyman made the trip. Much to his astonishment he discovered the grave, the husband, the children and all the current news.

The following Sunday he told the little five-year-old girl that the children were all well, that the husband had remarried pleasantly and that the grave was well kept.

She was very satisfied and thanked the clergyman very much—and the following Sunday could not recall a thing about it!

Past lives are not "reincarnation." That is a complex theory compared to simply living time after time, getting a new body, eventually losing it and getting a new one.

The facts of past lives, if you care to pursue them, are best done from a preclear's viewpoint in the hands of a competent Scientologist. The hypnotic handling of such is not advised. Only by higher levels of awareness does one learn, not deeper levels of unconsciousness.

An amusing sidelight on past lives is the "famous person" fixation. This more than anything else has discredited having lived before. There is always some madman "who was Napoleon," always some girl "who was Catherine the Great." This evidently means that the person, living a contemporary life to a famous figure, was so unsuccessful that he or she "dubbed-in" the great personage. A Scientologist who runs into "Beethoven," after the preclear has run it for a while, finds the preclear was really the handler of a street piano in that life—not Beethoven!

But all rules have exceptions and a Scientologist once found a preclear who claimed to have been Jim Bowie, the famous frontiersman who died at the doubly famous Alamo in Texas. And after much work and great skepticism found he really did have Jim Bowie!

People have also been animals and perhaps some animals have been people. There evidently is no gradient scale of advance as in the theories of reincarnation, but there are cases on record of preclears who got well after a life as a dog or other animal was run out by a Scientologist.

One case, a psychotic girl, recovered when a life as a lion who ate its keeper was fully run out!

And we have also known horses and dogs of "human intelligence." Perhaps they had just been generals or ministers of state and were taking it easy for a life or two to cure their ulcers!

Viewing children in the light of knowledge of past lives causes us to revise our estimations of causes of child behavior.

Evidently the newborn child has just died as an adult. Therefore he or she, for some years, is prone to fantasy and terror and needs a great deal of love and security to recover a perspective of life with which he or she can live.

Life is never dull in the researches and practice of Dianetics and Scientology. The motto is—*What is, is,* not what we wished it were.

London, England

Above The London Office of L. Ron Hubbard from where he wrote of cracking barriers to "whole track" memory in 1958

Right The first Hubbard Communications Office (HCO), where stood a first Organizational Chart

Far right top The Fitzroy Reception as it stood when serving as the first stable emanation point of L. Ron Hubbard communications worldwide

Far right bottom The HCO station from whence L. Ron Hubbard communications were transcribed and dispatched to far-flung outposts of Scientology through its formative years

London, England 109

35/37 Fitzroy Street, London, England: The original "Commonwealth Centre" of Scientology now similarly restored to stand as an LRH Heritage Site. It was here Ron headquartered both the Hubbard Association of Scientologists and the first Hubbard Communications Office for telex linkage to Scientology offices internationally. It was also here, between 1957 and 1959, he began the codification of a Scientology Bridge to immortality—*realized*.

CHAPTER SIX
THE BRIDGE

The Bridge

IN THE SIMPLEST (IF MOST EXPANSIVE) TERMS, L. RON HUBBARD describes Scientology as a Bridge from lower states of existence to far, far higher states. Below the Bridge lies an allegorical abyss of oblivion; atop lies unwavering immortality unto eternity. As one ascends the Bridge through successively higher states of awareness and ability, one literally transcends the "condition of human being" to arrive at a place only dimly described in literature of old. In that respect, Scientology becomes a religious experience in the most exalted sense, i.e., a complete spiritual transformation.

The imagery itself harkens back at least five thousand years and is dimly echoed in mainline mystical thought through both Asian and Western traditions. Implicit in the metaphor lies a journey that, while perilous, ultimately leads from grand illusion to stunning illumination. Hence, the Bridge as a broadly accessible and reliable path across a bottomless void to unending revelation. And hence the immensity of L. Ron Hubbard's track of discovery between 1959 and 1965.

The setting was his Saint Hill Manor estate at East Grinstead, Sussex, England. It has long loomed large in Scientology history and will forevermore. For it was here he cut the greater research trail while simultaneously delivering what is known today as the Saint Hill Special Briefing Course—being the chronological study of Scientology technical development and comprising some four hundred lectures detailing his investigatory trail. Accordingly, original Briefing Course

Left Saint Hill Manor, England, 1963

Left What will always be remembered as L. Ron Hubbard's home at Saint Hill Manor, Sussex, England, 1960

students walked but a short step behind Ron's developmental path as he hacked his way through the core of the reactive mind to stunning vistas of Clear and beyond. Thus, here was the culmination of all he envisioned when calling for a "better bridge" in the closing page of *Dianetics: The Modern Science of Mental Health*. And thus, this story comes full circle.

As a further word on circumstances and procedures, he tended to work through the nights in the third-floor Research Room affording a long view of the Saint Hill downs. Attendant staff would recall hearing a periodic "clink" of spent drawing pens dropping to a wastebasket, while reams of handwritten notes were waiting for typists in the mornings.

The most pertinent of which were transcribed into Technical Bulletins ultimately comprising some 350 issues to carefully delineate the actual procedures of progress. Included therein are all triggering mechanisms of human aberration both blatant and subtle. Also included are all potential pitfalls, traps and tripwires. In that regard, here was a map through a maze of enthralling mysteries that quite literally mesmerized human beings since the dawn of time.

Hence, the LRH dictum:

"This allegory is easily communicated and is quite true. Man has lacked, then, a bridge that any could travel. Scientology is the first bridge. It is complete, detailed and safe." ■

November 1965

THE STATES OF EXISTENCE

by L. Ron Hubbard

Man is so visibly Man that he overlooked in most of his philosophies and *all* of his sciences that there is more than one state of existence attainable by Man.

Indeed, until we came along and changed their minds, all nineteenth century psychologists *stated* that Man could never change. And described only one state of existence—mortal man.

If you think about it for a moment, you will see that there are many states of existence even in Man. He is rich or poor, well or sick, old or young, married or single. If Man can alter his state of existence as a man, could he be anything else than a man? Or a woman, or a boy or a girl?

There are two or more lower (and abhorrent) states of existence.

The state of ANIMAL is quite often descended to by Man as a chronic condition. Not only in mental hospitals, but in life, one can find such changes. Indeed, since 1870 the psychologists have said Man *was* an animal.

Man can also change to a state of matter. This is also seen in mental hospitals.

But those are lower states. Are there any upper and happier states?

These are the whole of the horizon and attainment of Scientology. We are *not* seeking to make the insane sane. We are seeking to make a Man into a higher being.

There are *many* states of existence besides that of Man. This has been touched on by earlier philosophies. What is new about Scientology is that one being can attain several different states of existence in just one lifetime.

This is so novel an outlook that it is no wonder Scientologists are sometimes misunderstood and are taken for healers or psychiatrists.

In fact, Man at large has never thought of it before. That he personally and in this lifetime could become something far higher and better than a Man is brand-new to him. He has heard of dying and his soul going to heaven or hell, and he has variously regarded the prospect as good or boring or terrifying.

But for John Doe to hear that he can become a higher being is a new thing.

Some savants amongst the Himalayas have worked in this direction. Gautama Siddhartha (Buddha) spoke of it. Fifteen or twenty years of hard work were said to result in a nebulous conclusion.

There are actually nine clear-cut states of existence higher than Homo sapiens.

A sick man would think the best possible states would be a well man or a dead man. And whereas these might be (to him) desirable states, they are still MAN.

Communication

The first state above MAN is a being who can communicate.

We instinctively revere the great artist, painter or musician and society as a whole looks upon them as not quite ordinary beings.

And they are not. They are a cut above Man. That they were born this way and were not audited to it does not make them less higher beings. He who can truly communicate to others is a higher being who builds new worlds.

Auditing can achieve this higher state of being—he or she who can communicate. That is a Grade 0 Release.

Problems

What distinguishes civilized Man as MAN is that he is mired into PROBLEMS which just get worse the more he "solves" them.

The being who can recognize the actual source of problems and so see them vanish is too rare to be easily comprehended. Man *solves* problems. A being in a higher state looks at them and they vanish.

There is fantastic phenomena here which MAN has never before Scientology examined.

When a being can do this—make problems vanish with a glance—he certainly is no longer MAN. And the problems artists have are legend.

A being can be audited up to being able to do this. It is a Grade I Release.

Relief

MAN has never known, except in some of the rare miracle workers he regarded as saints, how to bring relief to various ills.

The secret was that one is connecting oneself to what he abhors.

To be able to easily bring relief to oneself and others from the hostilities and sufferings of life is a skill MAN has seen only in healers.

Relief is obtained at Grade II Release.

The unveiling of the first Classification, Gradation and Awareness Chart, wherein all levels of the Scientology Bridge are delineated. It describes a gradient path to successively higher states of awareness and thus, in effect, becomes a road map to the Bridge.

Freedom

MAN is chained to the upsets in his past.

He has never understood why he felt so upset and misunderstood about his family or people or situations.

Most men dwell perpetually on troubles they have had. They lead sad lives.

Freedom from the upsets of the past with the ability to face the future is almost an unknown condition to MAN.

It is attained as a Grade III Release.

Ability

MAN's abilities tend to be individually specialized. He is so intent upon some action that he is clumsy in performing others.

Moving out of a fixed condition and being able to do other things is attained as a Grade IV Release.

Power

MAN can seldom handle POWER. He retreats from it or abuses it. When he has it he often misdirects it.

To have it and handle it is attained as a Grade V Release.

Whole Track Release

MAN is not even aware of his "time track." It is a record of his consecutive moments of living stretching back as long as he has lived.

His past is his "time track." There are three conditions concerning it. A being is first unaware he has one, then is fascinated by what he finds out about his own past and then finds what made him and it that way.

Some of this often shows up in lower auditing. But at this higher state one comes to handle it.

At this grade it is hard to describe the state, it is so high above common experience and is totally missing in all Man's literature.

It is Grade VI Release.

Clear

This state has often been described in Dianetics and Scientology. It has always been understated.

Release, for years, was mistaken for Clear and was even called Clear. But time has revealed that Clear was far above anything one had dreamed of previously.

Grade VII is not a Release Grade. It is a Clear.

Operating Thetan

This term "Operating Thetan," has meaning mainly to old-time Scientologists.

By "Operating" is meant "able to act and handle things" and by "Thetan" is meant the spiritual being that is the basic self. "Theta" is Greek for thought or Life or the spirit.

An Operating Thetan, then, is one who can handle things without having to use a body of physical means. "Poltergeist" is a learned term for only one of the phenomena of this state.

Basically, one is oneself, can handle things and exist without physical support or assistance.

This state is really just "OT" but is numbered Grade VIII for convenience. It doesn't mean one becomes God. It means one becomes wholly oneself.

Exterior

Since 1952 we have been able to make Man into a spiritual being in a few seconds.

It was startling. It was also unstable. A minute, a day or weeks later the person would become MAN again and the experience was often remembered only dimly.

Recently we solved why this was so. It is fatal to overrun the processes of a Grade once that Grade has been obtained. One can be audited on the processes of a new Grade one has not attained. But not on the same Grade one had already reached.

Overauditing—auditing beyond a Grade of Release attained—is very upsetting to a person. He often does not really know why he got upset. He got better, then got worse again.

The same thing happened with the "Thetan Exterior" processes. We made a person exteriorize and *then overaudited him* by a few more commands. Or the person tried to audit himself into further "exteriorization."

This state, however, is not a different state of existence. It occurs along with many of the higher Release Grades as a natural condition. And it is, of course, only a foreshadow of Operating Thetan.

Thus there are nine definite states of existence above that of Homo sapiens and there are some intermediate states such as Grade VA on the chart.

It is hard for Man to grasp even that these states exist. He has no literature about them really or any vocabulary for them.

But they do exist.

Reach for them and you'll see.

Once one starts going up, there is no wish to stop. The whiff of freedom and the total reality of it after all this time is too strong.

Scientology is concerned with the states above Man and opens the way with a certain and sure Bridge into a future. The way has been dreamed of in ages past. For Man it never existed until today.

And today we have it in Scientology.

A philosophy, declared L. Ron Hubbard, can only be a route to knowledge and if one possesses a route, then one can find what is true for oneself. Such is Scientology and such is the vantage point from which he authored "Philosophy Wins after 2,000 Years." Although self-explanatory, let us bear in mind the following: In referencing the pantheon of Greek philosophers, he is acknowledging the progenitors of Western logic, ethics, mathematics and transcendent wisdom. In discussing the decline of spiritual values in the face of material science, he is once more touching on the central plight of a modern Man who believes himself to be no more than chemical recombination. That he authored this statement in 1966 is especially significant; for it was then he commenced mapping the route to the state of Operating Thetan and thus that realm beyond realms "not even embraced by earlier literature."

LATE FEBRUARY 1966

PHILOSOPHY WINS AFTER 2,000 YEARS

by L. Ron Hubbard

PHILOSOPHY DID NOT DIE with Ancient Greece.

Out of the Natural Philosophy of those times came science.

The wonders of chrome and metal, cars, planes, the atom bomb and even the satellites have their roots in the firm base of Greek Philosophy.

But Socrates, Aristotle, Euclid, Thales, Heraclitus, Parmenides, Democritus, Pythagoras, Plato and all the rest did not have in mind the manufacture of material things when they released their knowledge to the world.

Even though all these great things developed out of Greek thought and mathematics, the great names of Philosophy considered they had failed.

And so they had. Until today.

For their philosophic goal was the understanding of the spirit of Man and his relationship to the Universe. And this they could only speculate upon. They never *proved* their contention that Man was a spirit clothed in flesh, they could only assert it.

And so they drowned in the avalanche of superstition which engulfed the world in the Dark Ages.

Why did they fail? They needed the higher mathematics and electronics which would, over two thousand years later, develop from their philosophies.

These *were* developed. But they were used for different purposes than those intended, and Man turned his back upon their lofty dreams while building planes to bomb cities and atom bombs to wipe out the Mankind no one had ever understood.

Until Scientology.

And in it the goals of Greek Philosophy live again.

The Greek Acropolis at Athens; photographs by L. Ron Hubbard,
1961: "Philosophy did not die with Ancient Greece" —LRH

The Acropolis, 1961: *"We have reached the star they saw. And we know what it is."* —LRH

Using modern developments in the sciences, it became possible to approach again the basic problems, What is Man? What is his relationship to the Universe? What is the Universe?

Scientology, after a third of a century of careful research and investigation, can answer, with scientific truth, those questions and can prove the answers.

This is rather startling.

We have come so far from Thales, Heraclitus, Parmenides and Democritus that we have almost forgotten what they were trying to discover. But if you consult writings of the work they did over two thousand years ago, you will see what it was.

They wanted Man to know. They did not fail. They laid the ancient Greeks a firm foundation on which to build. And two thousand and more years later, we can furnish all the evidence they need.

And that evidence and its truths and its great potential of betterment for the individual and all Mankind are completed work today in Scientology.

We have reached the star they saw. And we know what it is. You'll find its value when you become a Scientologist, a being who has come to know himself, life and the Universe and can give a hand to those around him to reach the stars.

Authored as a companion piece to "Philosophy Wins after 2,000 Years," Ron's 1966 "Scientology Answers" completes the statement: We have reached the star the ancients saw. That the vista presented here is a freedom quite beyond what philosophers of old imagined possible is more than a little significant; for here is a spiritual freedom one can experience whether one believes it or not, which is the whole point of Scientology.

LATE FEBRUARY 1966

SCIENTOLOGY ANSWERS

by L. Ron Hubbard

MAN HAS ASKED A great many questions about himself.

Such questions are "Who am I?" "Where do I come from?" "What is Death?" "Is there a Hereafter?"

Any child asks these questions, yet Man has never had answers that long satisfied him.

Religions have various answers to these questions and they belong in fact in the field of religious philosophy, since this is the area of Man's knowledge that has sought to answer them.

Answers have varied through the ages and race to race and this variation alone is the stumbling block which brings disbelief into faiths. Old religions fade because people no longer find their answers to the above questions real.

The decline of Christianity is marked by modern cynicism about a Hell where one burns for an eternity and a Heaven where one plays a harp forever.

Materialistic sciences have sought to invalidate the entire field by shrugging the problem off with the equally impossible answers that one is merely meat and all life arose by spontaneous and accidental combustion from a sea of ammonia. Such "answers" sound more like pre-Buddhist India where the world was said to be carried on seven elephants that stood on seven pillars which stood on a turtle and, in exasperation to the child's question as to what the turtle stood on, "Mud! And it's mud from there on down!"

It is the nature of Truth that if one knows it, even more things get understood. The disease and decay of Asia tends to invalidate their concepts as Truth and in the West, war, where soldiers saw "Gott Mit Uns" on the slain enemy belt buckles, tended to end the domination of the churches of those times—for God could not be on both sides of such Devil's work, or so the soldiers reasoned.

Athens as seen from the Acropolis, 1961

Even Christ's great commandment of "Love Thy Neighbor" seems to have less force today in a world of income tax, inflation and the slaughter of civil populations in the name of peace.

So without in any way condemning or scorning any man's beliefs, Scientology arose from the ashes of a spiritless science and again asked—and answered—the eternal questions.

That the answers have the force of Truth is attested by the results. Instead of the sickness of religious India, Scientologists are seldom ill. Instead of internal warfare such as the riots of Alexandria, Scientologists live in relative harmony with each other and have skills that restore relations rapidly.

The world tends to attack new things and Scientology has had its share from vested interest groups and governments but it keeps rising eventually victorious from each clash, without bitterness.

Various interesting results proceed from the practice of Scientology. One's intelligence increases and one's ability to handle his problems is markedly bettered.

One does not have to study Scientology very long to know that one does not have to die to find out what he is or where he is going after death, for *one can experience* it all for himself with no persuasion or hypnotism or "faith."

So Scientology is different mainly because one doesn't have to *believe* in it to have it work. Its truths are of the order of "Is this black?" "Is this white?" You can see for yourself something is black if it's black and that something is white when it's white. No tricks of logic are needed to prove any point and Scientologists only ask people to look for themselves.

Thus, along with science, Scientology can achieve positive invariable results. Given the same conditions, one always gets the same results. And anyone given the same conditions can obtain the same results.

What has happened is the *superstition* has been subtracted from spiritual studies. And today this is a very acceptable state of affairs to Man.

The ultimate freedom depends on knowing the ultimate Truth. Truth is not what people *say* it is, it is *what* it *is*. And Truth, quite remarkably, sets one free, just like philosophers have said down the ages.

What the philosophers did *not* say was how free can one get? And that is the surprise contained in Scientology for everyone who walks the Road to Truth—one *can* be totally free.

Naturally this makes no friendly news to the person who wants slaves and Fascistic, Capitalistic and even some more liberal creeds forbid that utterly, for who could be a master, so they think, where no slave wears his chains? They miss the point entirely, for who *has* to be a master?

When you yourself hold the Truth, the shadows by which you are bound tend to slither away.

And when you at last know for yourself in your own experience that Scientology does have the answers, and when you have applied them, you have the result all philosophers, savants, sages and saviors have always dreamed of—and freedom as well.

As much of Scientology is true for you as you know of it. Those who know it only by name react to the hope of it. And as one advances upon the road, one knows more and more of it and is more and

> *"For the first time in all the ages there is something that in this one lifetime delivers the answers to the eternal questions and delivers immortality as well."*

more free. Unlike so many promises made to Man and which have made him fear disappointment, Scientology delivers. It may be over a rough road. It may be over a smooth one. But Scientology eventually delivers all it says it can.

And that is what is new about it and why it grows. No other religion ever given Man delivered. They all waited until after the end for one to find his harp or his Nirvana.

For the first time in all the ages there *is* something that in this one lifetime delivers the answers to the eternal questions and delivers immortality as well.

With a recognition of our immortality, our essential goodness and inherent capabilities, Scientology became "a religious practice applying to Man's spirit and his spiritual freedom." It may be further defined as "the study and handling of the spirit in relationship to itself, universes and other life" and comprises "a wisdom in the tradition of ten thousand years of search in Asia and Western civilization."

Beyond these statements, no intellectual appreciation is sufficient. Given a thousand years of Christian doctrine, it is easy enough to form some conception of a Christian Heaven. While given the preponderance of the twenty-first-century scientific theory, it is even easier to imagine our lives in strictly material terms—striving for reasonable happiness until the neural cortex breaks down and we are plunged into absolute unconsciousness forever. But without some subjective experience, even L. Ron Hubbard, in this perfectly succinct 1966 explanation, can only suggest the "tremulous wonder" of all Scientology offers.

DECEMBER 1966

DIANETICS, SCIENTOLOGY AND BEYOND

by L. RON HUBBARD

FOR THOUSANDS OF YEARS men have sought the state of complete spiritual freedom from the endless cycle of birth and death and have sought personal immortality containing full awareness, memory and ability as a spirit independent of the flesh.

The dream of this in Buddha's time was called "Bodhi," being the name of the tree under which he attained such a state.

But due to the unknown presence of the reactive mind and its effect upon the spirit as well as the body, such periods of freedom were difficult to attain and were, as we have found, temporary.

Further, few could attain even this temporary state and those who did acquired it at the cost of decades of self-denial and personal discipline.

In Scientology, this state has been attained. It has been achieved not on a temporary basis, subject to relapse, but on a stable plane of full awareness and ability, unqualified by accident or deterioration. And not limited to a few.

By eradicating the reactive mind we not only achieve, in the state of Clear, an erasure of the seeming evil in Man, who is basically good, we have overcome the barriers which made it so difficult to attain total spiritual independence and serenity.

We call this state "Operating Thetan." To *operate* something is to be able to handle it. *Thetan* is from the Greek letter "theta," the traditional philosopher's symbol (from the letter in the Greek alphabet "theta," θ) of thought, spirit or life. Thus it means a being who as a spirit alone can handle things.

The definition of the state of Operating Thetan is "Knowing and willing cause over Life, Thought, Matter, Energy, Space and Time."

The legendary Porch of Maidens, Athens, Greece, 1961:
"Thetan is from the Greek letter 'theta,' the traditional philosopher's symbol of thought, spirit or life" —LRH

As Man is basically good, despite his evil reactions to his reactive mind, a being who is Clear becomes willing to trust himself with such abilities. And in any case, none can have more power than they can control.

In Scientology, a Clear can walk his way to Operating Thetan, not in the decades demanded even by a temporary state in past ages, but within months or at most a year or so. And when he attains the state he is no longer subject to sudden and inexplicable collapses as occurred 2,500 years ago. One is able to attain and retain the desirable condition.

Not the least of the qualities of OT is personal and knowing immortality and freedom from the cycle of birth and death.

The concept is rather vast for immediate grasp, but chiefly because one has hoped and had his hope for this turned to despair and his despair turned to a total apathy, concerning it, too often down the ages to do more than extend a tremulous wonder.

But the way is true and plainly marked and all one needs to do is to place his feet upon the first rung of the ladder of Dianetics, ascend by Scientology to Clear and then walk upward to and far beyond the stars.

It is quite impossible to overstate the importance of such news. 2,500 years ago, a statement similar to this and almost impossible to attain brought civilization to three-quarters of Asia.

Yet day by day, Clears enrolled on the "OT Course" at Saint Hill are walking that ladder and have already begun to reach the stars.

It is quite true. And quite attainable on the well-marked road of modern Scientology.

When considering all Dianetics and Scientology represent to the everyday man and forgotten man, it is hardly surprising L. Ron Hubbard would have met opposition. In the simplest terms, he speaks of a Power Elite made uneasy by a movement wherein "the little people of the world, endure and turn into philosophers overnight, unaffected suddenly by the dismal threats of their 'betters.'" In somewhat greater detail, he also speaks of an international psychiatric community at loggerheads to any spiritual movement for individual liberty, particularly one that measurably raises intelligence and ability. Then again, he speaks of a psychiatric-intelligence effort to not only bury Scientology but to seize it... And the record bears him out.

But the overriding point is encapsulated in what we present here with L. Ron Hubbard's "My Only Defense for Having Lived." It dates from 1966, or when a renegade British intelligence conspired with a then apartheid Southern African government to keep LRH literacy tools out of black African schools and thereby preserve white dominance of the diamond mines. Deeply personal and immensely powerful, let us further describe it as a statement from a man whose life cannot be divorced from his philosophic convictions.

15 August 1966

MY ONLY DEFENSE FOR HAVING LIVED

by L. Ron Hubbard

THE ONLY TESTS OF a life well lived are: Did he do what he intended? and Were people glad he lived?

People have often desired me to write an autobiography and while I would be perfectly willing to do so had I the time, I consider such a work, as I do myself, quite unimportant. I have led an adventurous life and it would possibly be entertaining to read, but I doubt such a work would shed any background light on my researches and would not clarify my intentions or why I developed Dianetics and Scientology.

My motives have not been fame. I tried to give *Dianetics,* the entire work, to the American Medical Association and the American Psychiatric Association in 1949 and the AMA only said, "Why should you?" and the APA said, "If it is important, we will hear of it." I tried to avoid, until July 1950, saying I had personally done the research, but then owned to it when I saw that unowned it could be lost in its original form.

My motives have not included amassing great wealth. The royalties of the First Book, *Dianetics: The Modern Science of Mental Health,* were given to the first Foundation. So it is not wealth.

Power has not been my motive. I only held office in organizations to insist upon correct usage of the work and, this having been achieved sometime since, I resigned all directorships and retained only an honorary post. Further, one cannot have more power than he himself already has as a being; so power by reason of position I consider pointless and a waste of time.

My motives are so hard to understand because they largely omit me from the equation. And self-centered men are not likely to understand such a thing since *they* know they would not forego fame, wealth or power and so conceive that another would not.

To try to understand me or Scientology by recounting the adventures of my life is a rather unrelated action. I am myself, not my adventures. I have gone through the world studying Man in order to understand him and *he,* not my adventures in doing so, is the important thing.

I always operated on the somewhat naive idea that my life was my own, to be lived as best I could. A life is not always easy to live. When one's life becomes "public property," as mine seems to have done, one is ill-prepared and not even inclined to explain it all. It has been lived, it cannot be unlived and there it is. The *results* of having lived at all, then, are the only things that count.

I never considered it worthwhile to live believably as that is a compromise which denies one's own integrity.

Also, to try to explain the technical inventions of a scientist by the way he plays a mandolin is of course something only a very dull person would do—yet of course people so try.

The trouble with my life is that it has been adventurous and would make, perhaps, interesting reading to lovers of adventure stories.

One does not study Man successfully from an ivory tower and part of my intentions has been to live a very full life in many strata so as to understand Man. And this I have done.

I cannot say that I have liked all the things men do and say. But I can say that despite many reasons not to, I have persevered in helping Man all I could and continuing his friend.

Long since I ceased to talk about my real life. I learned long ago that man has his standards of credulity and when reality clashes with these he feels challenged.

For instance, I could read and write when I was three and a half. I could read minds and foretell the future with great accuracy. Such accomplishments startle people and I early learned in this lifetime to keep my own actual abilities to myself or else find sociability impossible.

I grew up on the frontier amid brute force and the worship of brawn, learned to live in such a rough and tumble world, not die in forty-below blizzards or lose my own standards in a barbarous society where agony was amusing to the people. It carried its own legends and I had my adventures, but I learned to tell the lesser tale.

No more than acclimatized in this lifetime to the Old West, I found myself moved to the South Pacific and Asia, to a world of courtesy and soft ways, and had to adopt a new pattern of survival.

This was no more than learned than I found myself, against my will, in the collegiate world studying engineering and mathematics and learned new lessons in social contact. In this I was quite successful, becoming the head of various college clubs and societies. But in adapting a dead mathematics to new modern uses, I so assaulted the prejudices of my professors, who thought dead mathematics should have no use, that I learned once more about our world. I was ridiculed or frowned upon too often for writing or looking for the truth to ever conceive much love for the artificial towers of learning—so aloof from life. I decided to go study other races and organized an expedition and set sail in an old four-mast schooner rather than carry on longer in the academic world. I am amused to be condemned by some for not having studied in college a subject which was not taught there and which I had to develop to fill the gap in Man's knowledge of himself. The answers did not exist in the books of philosophy I studied. It had to be looked for in the real world.

I wrote, I lived, I travelled, I prospered, I learned. I unfortunately could not quite help doing spectacular things. They would not look spectacular to me until I saw them in the eyes of others. And so I began to work very hard to tell the lesser tale, to do what I must to learn about Man and help him as I could and yet not see wide-eyed disbelief, even shock, when someone at the Explorers Club

would introduce me as having roped a Kodiak bear, having climbed a volcano to see its eruption at close hand or as the doer of some other feat. I became cautious in my anecdotes, but I was looking at and living life, in order to experience it and what happened to *me* was entirely secondary.

When you see a student body of would-be writers almost mob you for saying factually you wrote a hundred thousand words a month as a quota, when you tell what is to you a simple truth and yet find others consider it extraordinary beyond belief, you grow cautious about retelling the consecutive incidents which are your day by day life. You conclude others don't have a day by day life like that and so, not wanting to seem strange, you simply say less. And when you do say, you tell what you hope is ordinary and mildly entertaining.

Background for autobiography abounds. But who would read it as an honest tale and so I have not written it and never will. It would sound far, far too incredible. So I have abstained from writing vast tomes about myself and my adventures, not because I had done anything bad, but because it was not important to do so and nobody would even believe my tales anyway.

Thus I have left a bit of mystery, unintentional, that others, with bad intent can fill in from their imaginations. I did not intend it so.

My intentions in life did not include making a story of myself. I only wanted to know Man and understand him. I did not really care if he did not understand me so long as he understood himself. I was the lesser part of my project. Some say this is unfortunate, but I do not find it so. I did not live to be understood, but to understand.

And it does not matter. Long ago I ceased utterly to defend myself against lies and calumny where it occurred. To some this will be considered strange. But how can one control the vaporings of a press which never interviews one?

Does one condemn and fight each rumor or lie? I long ago realized I had not the time. But mainly I had not the inclination to stop Man's speech and punish him for being what he was and for thinking what he did.

I learned early the folly of fighting the viciously inclined. I was once expelled from an island, as a boy, by a gloomy and brooding governor on a charge of always being happy and smiling. There was no more story than that.

So what does one do? Does one seek vengeance and death on men because they are ignorant, dull or intolerant?

Not when one's mission is to understand and help men.

Does one defend oneself against lies and infamy when one is already too busy doing his job?

One chooses what one is to do. And does it. All else is foolish distraction.

Threats to myself are unimportant in the scheme of things. I knew I would attain my goals. I knew it a long time ago.

I only once was frightened by the immensity of the implications of understanding Man. It was when I had isolated in the late thirties what appeared to be the Dynamic Principle of Existence and knew where such a discovery would lead. I remembered Man habitually crucified anyone who brought him wisdom or truly helped him.

I was frightened for a bit. But I realized I had searched for an answer for too many years already to give up now. And then I accepted that condition. And have not halted on my way because of personal fear.

My life's history has no import. I have lived. My only real regrets have been killing men in the thunder and passion of war and though I wish I had not, still it was done.

What people say I as a being have or have not done has no bearing on the fact that my work has been done, done well and lives to help Man become a better being. If I personally triumph for it or die for it in this life is not of the slightest possible importance.

What I have done for Man's use cannot be undone by thousands of hostile columns of press or a hundred billion slanderous lies. My friends, and I have many, know they are lies, which is quite enough.

I am myself. I can hold up my head to myself. I know what I have done in developing a new philosophy and certainly I am not so foolish as to suppose it has no consequences for me. Only a fool would expect or value praise from the insane and not expect damage from the act of attempting to assist a wounded wild animal. One takes the consequences with the act.

I have carried out my basic intention—to understand Man and help him attain greater heights of civilization through knowledge of himself.

And any friend I have and many, many more are glad that I have lived.

And that is the story of my life—the only story that matters.

My adventures, my heartbreaks, the joy I take in the singing wind and sea, my pride in creating prose and pictures, my attempts to compose music, my laughter with my friends and likes, dislikes and deeds are none of them discreditable. So there have been attacks. Need this startle anyone? Such actions only prove that Man needs help and needs it badly if he attacks his friends.

A past researched relentlessly for sixteen years by the world's press and even the police of a planet without the discovery of a single crime must be a singularly unstained past indeed!

Were you to read the press up to 1950, I was a mildly famous, colorful person of excellent family, of unblemished repute, a member of famous clubs and societies, with many friends in high places. On the publication of a book concerning the mind, I suddenly overnight was a

dark villain with a terrible past (the crimes of course unspecified, since there were none). From this we only learn that a person's own mind is apparently a monopoly somewhere, property of a sensitive group that profits too much to lose control. In any year thousands of books are written on philosophy and the mind, many banal, many vicious, many harmful, with no protest from anyone. Many of such works are by important people. In any year thousands of self-betterment groups, good and evil, are formed without comment. Why then did the publications of a book and the forming of a foundation cause such a fantastic reaction, all out of proportion to the importance of such usual acts? Could it be because no special-interest group had this new subject under their control? Could it be because the new subject had in it too much power of truth? How is it that for sixteen years, at this writing, the work, the groups have continued and multiplied in the face of all opposition, including that of governments (whose actions are startling as who revolted against them)?

I sometimes feel like an old-time explorer, offering a balm to a pygmy mother for her baby's skin rash, and being fearfully hunted by the tribe for "trying to put a spell on them." Ah well, explorers ran into that, didn't they?

With this much violence, had there been anything wrong with my past, or with my current activities, I long since would have been done away with by the normal processes of law. But no, I remained untouched for all those sixteen years.

It has not been easy to live and work in a hostile atmosphere and yet protect my family and to carry on and keep faith with those who trusted me. I have borne it for the sake of others and for Man. It is interesting that all attempted actions against Scientology have eventually failed and have been proven falsely based in any court of law.

My Only Defense for Having Lived

But who is this that is denounced by mighty figures of the press, by men of towering importance in the governments of the planet, who must be lied about and somehow put down? I as a person am not that important.

It doesn't make sense. And it makes less sense the more you consider it. For neither I nor the subject is an enemy of any of them.

Being easy in my own mind and sincere in the help I offered Man and in my interest in him and in being at least one friend in a lonely world, I am not of course going to engage upon an impassioned defense of myself or much less engage in violent attacks upon the rather less than sane people who make such senseless (and nebulous) charges.

Dianetics and Scientology are perfectly plain to anyone who studies and uses them. No matter what adventures I have had, Scientology is not unbelievable. A six-year-old boy, just last night, graduated from a Communications Course and was *very* happy about it as life looked so much easier to him now. Anyone who studies the technology finds it helps Man communicate, solve his problems, become a more social being, makes it unnecessary for him to continue to excuse his failures with more failures and frees him as a spiritual being. Man and philosophers have been hoping and trying to do these things all down the ages. Why the charges of villainy when it has at last become possible for any person to follow an easy way to freedom and have a saner, happier civilization?

But then one remembers that philosophers have been given hemlock and that others who tried to help Man have been slain in fury and one begins to see that it is a dangerous activity. Only a being with the highest possible sense of adventure and dedication would ever attempt to solve the riddle of Man's being and destiny. The most incredible adventure of all was to advance a solution to that riddle. For the hiding place is strewn with the bones of those who tried in ages past, all far better men than I.

So only a chap with nerve enough to walk unarmed amongst savages in far places would ever seek to solve the riddle of existence. That by now is obvious!

To me the only important thing is that I have finished and written my work. Despite all that I have done.

And Man, despite anything he now says or does, may someday be glad that I have lived.

Let that suffice.

It is the only important thing.

I only hope that I have helped.

I have done my job. This no man in truth will ever be able to decry. How important that job was is for the future, not for me, to decide.

Given all we have presented here reflects a personal philosophic conviction, let us also now present L. Ron Hubbard's "My Philosophy." Dating from the spring of 1965, the work has been rightly described as the definitive LRH statement on his philosophic stance. Although no other explanation is necessary, the following may be of interest: In alluding to injuries suffered through the Second World War, he is referencing wounds sustained in combat on the island of Java and aboard a corvette in the North Atlantic. In noting his abandonment as of 1945, he is citing a sad and all-too-common fate of returning American soldiers, i.e., the reluctance of families, and wives in particular, to assume the burden of crippled veterans; hence the rash of postwar divorces. Finally, and lest it is not already obvious, all sentiments expressed here were lifelong, and he did, indeed, continue "writing and working and teaching so long as I exist."

My Philosophy
by
L Ron Hubbard

The subject of philosophy is very ancient. The word means "the love, study or pursuit of wisdom, or of knowledge of things and their causes, whether theoretical or practical."

MY PHILOSOPHY

by L. Ron Hubbard

The subject of philosophy is very ancient. The word means "the love, study or pursuit of wisdom, or of knowledge of things and their causes, whether theoretical or practical."

All we know of science or of religion comes from philosophy. It lies behind and above all other knowledge we have or use.

For long regarded as a subject reserved for halls of learning and the intellectual, the subject to a remarkable degree has been denied the man in the street.

Surrounded by protective coatings of impenetrable scholarliness, philosophy has been reserved to the privileged few.

The first principle of my own philosophy is that wisdom is meant for anyone who wishes to reach for it. It is the servant of the commoner and king alike and should never be regarded with awe.

Selfish scholars seldom forgive anyone who seeks to break down the walls of mystery and let the people in. Will Durant, the modern American philosopher, was relegated to the scrapheap by his fellow scholars when he wrote a popular book on the subject, *The Story of Philosophy*. Thus brickbats come the way of any who seek to bring wisdom to the people over the objections of the "inner circle."

The second principle of my own philosophy is that it must be capable of being applied.

Learning locked in mildewed books is of little use to anyone and therefore of no value unless it can be used.

The third principle is that any philosophic knowledge is only valuable if it is true or if it works.

These three principles are so strange to the field of philosophy that I have given my philosophy a name: *Scientology*. This means only "knowing how to know."

A philosophy can only be a *route* to knowledge. It cannot be knowledge crammed down one's throat. If one has a route, he can then find what is true for him. And that is Scientology.

Original handwritten page from
L. Ron Hubbard's "My Philosophy"

Above
Saint Hill Manor, 1966: "Since 1950 I have had Mankind knocking on my door. It has not mattered where I have lived or how remote. Since I first published a book on the subject, my life has no longer been my own."
—LRH

Know thyself—and the truth shall set you free.

Therefore, in Scientology we are not concerned with individual actions and differences. We are only concerned with how to show Man how he can set himself or herself free.

This, of course, is not very popular with those who depend upon the slavery of others for their living or power. But it happens to be the only way I have found that really improves an individual's life.

Suppression and oppression are the basic causes of depression. If you relieve those, a person can lift his head, become well, become happy with life.

And though it may be unpopular with the slave master, it is very popular with the people. Common Man likes to be happy and well. He likes to be able to understand things. And he knows his route to freedom lies through knowledge.

Therefore, since 1950 I have had Mankind knocking on my door. It has not mattered where I have lived or how remote. Since I first published a book* on the subject, my life has no longer been my own.

I like to help others and count it as my greatest pleasure in life to see a person free himself of the shadows which darken his days.

These shadows look so thick to him and weigh him down so that when he finds they *are* shadows and that he can see through them, walk through them and be again in the sun, he is enormously delighted. And I am afraid I am just as delighted as he is.

* Dianetics: The Modern Science of Mental Health, published in May 1950.

THE L. RON HUBBARD SERIES | *Philosopher & Founder*

I have seen much human misery. As a very young man I wandered through Asia and saw the agony and misery of overpopulated and undereducated lands. I have seen people uncaring and stepping over dying men in the streets. I have seen children less than rags and bones. And amongst this poverty and degradation I found holy places where wisdom was great but where it was carefully hidden and given out only as superstition. Later, in Western universities, I saw Man obsessed with materiality and with all his cunning, I saw him hide what little wisdom he really had in forbidding halls and make it inaccessible to the common and less favored man. I have been through a terrible war and saw its terror and pain uneased by a single word of decency or humanity. I have lived no cloistered life and hold in contempt the wise man who has not *lived* and the scholar who will not share.

There have been many wiser men than I, but few have traveled as much road.

I have seen life from the top down and the bottom up. I know how it looks both ways. And I know there *is* wisdom and that there is hope.

Blinded with injured optic nerves and lame with physical injuries to hip and back at the end of World War II, I faced an almost nonexistent future. My service record states, "This officer has no neurotic or psychotic tendencies of any kind whatsoever," but it also states, "permanently disabled physically." And so there came a further blow—I was abandoned by family and friends as a supposedly hopeless cripple and a probable burden upon them for the rest of my days. I yet worked my way back to fitness and strength in less than two years using only what I knew and could determine about Man and his relationship to the universe. I had no one to help me; what I had to know I had to find out. And it's quite a trick studying when you cannot see. I became used to being told it was all impossible, that there was no way, no hope. Yet I came to see again and walk again and I built an entirely new life. It is a happy life, a busy one and I hope a useful one. My only moments of sadness are those which come when bigoted men tell others all is bad and there is no route anywhere, no hope anywhere, nothing but sadness and sameness and desolation and that every effort to help others is false. I know it is not true.

So my own philosophy is that one should share what wisdom he has, one should help others to help themselves and one should keep going despite heavy weather, for there is always a calm ahead. One should also ignore catcalls from the selfish intellectual who cries, "Don't expose the mystery. Keep it all for ourselves. The people cannot understand."

But as I have never seen wisdom do any good kept to oneself, and as I like to see others happy, and as I find the vast majority of the people can and *do* understand, I will keep on writing and working and teaching so long as I exist.

For I know no man who has any monopoly upon the wisdom of this universe. It belongs to those who can use it to help themselves and others.

If things were a little better known and understood, we would all lead happier lives.

And there is a way to know them and there *is* a way to freedom.

The old must give way to the new, falsehood must become exposed by truth, and truth, though fought, always in the end prevails.

Saint Hill, England

Above The L. Ron Hubbard Office at Saint Hill Manor—everlasting symbol of his presence. It was here he left behind both a Scientology Bridge to ultimate freedom and Scientology organizations to carry the weight of the spanning.

Right Ron's Saint Hill desk from whence came so many defining statements of Dianetics and Scientology, very much including "My Only Defense for Having Lived" and "My Philosophy"

Far right top Saint Hill Auditing Demonstration Room: it was from here Ron's closed-circuit Scientology auditing demonstrations were televised to students of the first Saint Hill Special Briefing Course… Which is to say, it was here the technical perfection of Scientology application came to fruition as he mapped a hairline path through the reactive mind.

Far right bottom Saint Hill Research Room, where, through the latter months of 1965, Ron extended the Scientology Bridge to states of "full awareness, memory and ability as a spirit independent of the flesh"

Saint Hill, England 151

Saint Hill Manor, East Grinstead, Sussex, England: the perennial home of L. Ron Hubbard. Now restored to that moment of glory in 1965, visitors may again walk the rooms Ron walked when forging the scope and structure of Scientology.

Saint Hill, England 153

Epilogue

Since the announcement of philosophic principles discussed in this publication, Scientology has become the fastest-growing religious movement on Earth. To date, some ten thousand new adherents step onto the Scientology Bridge every week, while hundreds of new Scientology organizations open doors to meet their needs. Scientology has further become this century's most broadly inclusive movement, embracing those from every denomination and every faith, and altogether underscoring L. Ron Hubbard's pronouncement "Wisdom is meant for anyone who wishes to reach for it."

Yet what is ultimately most important here is what lies behind the growth of Scientology. Philosophy, we have stated, is the love of wisdom or pursuit of wisdom, and in that respect Scientology stands in a genuinely ancient tradition. But what Scientology offers, what it represents as a route to freedom—this is wholly new. For suddenly, in this otherwise desolate age, here is a truly workable philosophy that is absolutely relevant to every aspect of our lives and all of it follows from L. Ron Hubbard's crucial declaration:

We are studying the soul or spirit.

We are studying it as itself.

We are not trying to use this study

to enhance some other study or belief.

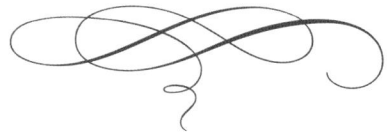

APPENDIX

Glossary | 159
Index | 217

GLOSSARY

A

abates: diminishes or reduces in intensity, amount, etc. Page 105.

aberrated: affected by *aberration,* any deviation or departure from rationality. Page 37.

aberration: any deviation or departure from rationality. Used in Dianetics to include psychoses, neuroses, compulsions and repressions of all kinds and classifications. From the Latin, *aberrare,* to wander from; Latin, *ab,* away, *errare,* to wander. It means basically to err, to make mistakes, or more specifically to have fixed ideas which are not true. The word is also used in its scientific sense. It means departure from a straight line. If a line should go from A to B, then if it is "aberrated" it would go from A to some other point, to some other point, to some other point, to some other point, to some other point and finally arrive at B. Taken in its scientific sense, it would also mean the lack of straightness or to see crookedly as, in example, a man sees a horse but thinks he sees an elephant. Page 35.

abhorrent: causing one to shrink with horror; causing utter dislike, inspiring disgust. Page 119.

abhors: dislikes or rejects (something or someone) very strongly. Page 120.

abiding: continuing without change; enduring; lasting. Page 18.

abolishing: putting an end to; doing away with completely. Page 62.

abounds: exists in great quantity. Page 140.

abstained: held back voluntarily from doing something. Page 140.

abstract: an idea or term considered apart from some material basis or object. Page 25.

abyss: a vast or bottomless opening, void space, etc., thought of as leading to or containing something immensely harmful, destructive, etc. Page 115.

academic: 1. of or relating to a school or other educational institutions; scholastic; scholarly. Page 2.
2. merely theoretical; involved in study rather than practical application. Page 9.

accessible: easy to approach, reach, enter, use, etc. Page 115.

acclimatized: accustomed to an environment, situation or the like. Page 139.

Acropolis: the elevated, fortified section of the city of Athens, Greece. Beginning in the fifth century B.C., the Greeks built a series of structures there, including a temple dedicated to the city's patron goddess, Athena, and several theaters. Page 125.

add up: formulate an opinion of or conclusion of; make sense of. Page 88.

adherents: those devoted to or supportive of a person, party or system; followers. Page 1.

admonitions: advices or warnings. Page 25.

Adrenalin: a substance prepared synthetically and used as a heart stimulant. The same substance is also a hormone (usually spelled *adrenaline*) that the body produces and releases into the bloodstream in response to physical or mental stress, as from fear of injury. Besides stimulating heart action, it initiates other bodily responses, such as increase in blood pressure. Page 84.

advent: arrival of something important. Page 7.

aesthetics: the study or theory of beauty and responses to it; specifically, the branch of philosophy dealing with art, its creative sources, its forms and its effects. Page 68.

afflicted: seriously affected or troubled; suffering. Page 52.

afford: supply or provide something. Page 70.

affront: a personally offensive act or words; deliberate act or display of disrespect; insult. Page 79.

Alamo: a reference to the battle that took place in Texas in 1836 at the *Alamo*, an old Roman Catholic mission used as a fort. For thirteen days, two thousand Mexican troops surrounded 187 Texans, until the Texans ran low on ammunition, at which point the Mexicans broke into the fort and killed the defenders. Page 106.

albeit: although; even if. Page 33.

Alexandria: a city and seaport in northern Egypt, founded in 332 B.C. by military general and king of Macedonia, Alexander the Great (356–323 B.C.). In ancient times the city was the site of brutal conflicts between opposing Christian sects, resulting in mass slaughters of the city's inhabitants. Page 130.

all but: almost; very nearly. Page 56.

allegorical: expressing something as a symbolic representation of, rather than the thing itself. Page 115.

aloof: not involved; at a distance from. Page 139.

AMA: an abbreviation for *American Medical Association.* Page 137.

amalgamated: combined to form a unified or integrated whole. Page 100.

amassing: gathering for oneself; accumulating (a large amount of something) over a period of time. Page 137.

American Fiction Guild: a national organization of magazine fiction writers and novelists in the United States in the 1930s. L. Ron Hubbard was the president of the New York chapter in 1936. (A *guild* is an organization of persons with related interests, goals, etc., especially one formed for mutual aid or protection.) Page 89.

American Medical Association: a professional physicians' organization in the United States, founded in 1847 and composed of state and county medical associations. Page 137.

American Psychiatric Association: national society of psychiatrists founded in 1844 as the Association of Medical Superintendents of American Institutions for the Insane. Page 137.

amnesia: a partial or total loss of memory. Page 105.

Ampex: a major American manufacturer of audio, video and magnetic tape products, audio recorders, radio and television equipment, etc., founded in 1944 by Russian-born engineer Alexander M. Poniatoff (1892–1980). Page 92.

analytical mind: that mind which computes—the "I" and his consciousness. Page 40.

Anaximander: sixth-century B.C. Greek philosopher and astronomer, author of one of the earliest works on the universe and the origins of life. Page 22.

ancestral bird: belonging to a former, or the earliest, generation (of a particular bird). Page 10.

Ancient Greece: a civilization that thrived around the Mediterranean Sea from circa 3000 B.C. to the first century B.C., known for advances in philosophy, architecture, drama, government and science. The most famous period of ancient Greek civilization (the Classical Age) lasted from about 480 to 323 B.C. During this period, ancient Greeks reached their highest prosperity and produced their highest cultural accomplishments. Page 125.

anecdote: a short account of a particular incident or event of an interesting or amusing nature, often biographical. Page 140.

Anglo-Irish: of English origin or descent and living in Ireland, or of mixed English and Irish ancestry. Page 18.

animal kingdom: one of the three broad divisions of natural objects: the animal, vegetable and mineral kingdoms. A *kingdom* is a region or sphere of nature. Page 42.

APA: an abbreviation for *American Psychiatric Association.* Page 137.

apartheid: (in the Republic of South Africa) a rigid policy of political and economic discrimination and segregation of the nonwhite population, in effect from 1948 to 1991. Page 136.

appropriate: to take without permission or consent; seize. Page 7.

Arabian Nights: or *A Thousand and One Nights,* a collection of stories from Persia, Arabia, India and Egypt, compiled over hundreds of years. They include the stories of Aladdin and Ali Baba and have become particularly popular in Western countries. Page 13.

arcane: understood by few; mysterious. Page 18.

Aristarchus: (310?–250? B.C.) Greek astronomer, the first to state that the Earth rotates and also revolves around the Sun. Page 20.

Aristotle: (384–322 B.C.) Greek philosopher, educator and scientist. His works covered all branches of human knowledge known in his time, including logic, ethics, natural science and politics. Page 20.

artifact: anything made by human art and workmanship. Page 44.

artificial towers: variation of *ivory towers.* An *ivory tower* is a figurative reference to a separation from real-life problems; a state or situation in which somebody is sheltered from the practicalities or difficulties of ordinary life. Page 139.

ascend: rise to a higher state, level or position. Page 115.

aspect(s): one side or part of something; a facet, phase or part of a whole. Page 41.

aspired: directed one's hopes or ambitions toward achieving something. Page 65.

assaulted: violently attacked with nonphysical weapons (as words, arguments or appeals). Page 139.

assist: a simple, easily done process (a systematic and technically exact series of steps, actions or changes to bring about a specific and definite result) that can be applied to anyone to help them recover more rapidly from accidents, mild illness or upsets. Page 51.

Astounding Science Fiction: a magazine founded in 1930 that featured adventure stories and, later, science fiction. The May 1950 issue featured one of the first articles on Dianetics, *Dianetics: The Evolution of a Science.* Page 18.

astronomy: the scientific study of the universe and the bodies, gas and dust within it. Astronomy includes observations and theories about the solar system, the stars, the galaxies and the general structure of space. Page 19.

Athens: the capital and largest city of Greece, situated in the southeastern part of the country. Athens has been a center of Greek culture since the fifth century B.C. Page 125.

at length: in detail. Page 42.

atom disintegrator: something that separates or breaks down atoms into smaller particles. Page 24.

atom(s): the smallest unit of any chemical element, consisting of a positive nucleus surrounded by negative electrons. For philosophers in ancient times, the *atom* was the basic particle of matter, indestructible and indivisible, regarded as the fundamental component of the universe. Page 22.

atom, splitting the: the splitting of atomic nuclei (the central region of atoms, consisting of minute, tightly bound particles and containing most of the mass) and the subsequent release of vast amounts of energy as observed in a nuclear reaction. In the early 1930s, scientists in Cambridge, England, became the first to split the atom. Page 23.

auditing: the application of Dianetics and Scientology techniques (called *processes*). Processes are directly concerned with increasing the ability of the individual to survive, with increasing his sanity or ability to reason, his physical ability and his general enjoyment of life. Also called *processing*. Page 2.

aversion: an intense or definite feeling of dislike. Page 100.

axioms: statements of natural laws on the order of those of the physical sciences. Page 1.

B

bacterial: consisting of *bacteria,* single-celled microorganisms (organisms so small that they can only be seen under a microscope). Page 9.

balm: a fragrant, oily substance obtained from various plants, such as evergreen trees, used in soothing ointments or other preparations. Page 143.

banal: common; ordinary. Page 143.

bank(s): a storage place for information, as in early computers where data was stored on a group or series of cards called a bank. Page 39.

banner: a guiding principle, cause or philosophy, from the literal meaning of *banner,* a flag on a pole, such as one used in battle by a country or a king. Page 53.

banner headlines: headlines extending across the width of a newspaper page, usually across the top of the front page. Literally, a *banner* is a long strip of cloth with an advertisement, greeting, etc., lettered on it. Page 100.

bar: obstruct, prevent, hinder or impede. Page 40.

barbarous: uncivilized, crude or savage. Page 139.

Bay Head: a town on the Atlantic coast of the United States, in the state of New Jersey, about 70 miles (110 kilometers) south of New York City. Page 33.

beachfront: located on or adjacent to a beach. Page 33.

bear in mind: keep an idea fixed in the memory or in one's thoughts, often as a cautionary measure or a reminder of something important; remember to take something into consideration. *Bear* here means hold or carry. Page 124.

bears out: shows to be true; supports or confirms. Page 136.

bears upon: relates to or affects something. Page 52.

Beethoven: Ludwig van Beethoven (1770–1827), German composer. Before Beethoven, composers wrote works for religious services, to teach and to entertain people at social functions. He was the first composer that people listened to just for the sake of listening to the music. Page 106.

behavioral: of or relating to *behaviorism,* an approach to the study of psychology that concentrates exclusively on observing, measuring and modifying behavior. Page 9.

Berkeley, George: (1685–1753) Anglo-Irish philosopher and clergyman who held that there is no separate external world and that matter does not exist independent of the mind that perceives it. However, he said, things can exist that are not immediately perceived by any human being because everything exists in the mind of God, who perceives all things. Page 18.

betters: persons who are superior to others in some way, as in position or authority, etc. Page 136.

bigoted: utterly intolerant of any creed, belief or opinion that differs from one's own. Page 149.

biochemical: of or pertaining to the science dealing with the chemical substances, processes and reactions that occur in living organisms. Page 10.

Blackfeet: a group of Native North American peoples including the Blackfeet of Montana and several tribes now living in Canada. This group controlled areas that were fought over by fur traders in the 1800s. Page 75.

blackjack: a gambling game at cards in which any player wins who gets cards totaling twenty-one points or less while the dealer gets either a smaller total or a total exceeding twenty-one points. Also called *twenty-one.* Page 84.

blatant: done in an open and obvious way; outright. Page 117.

blizzard: a severe snowstorm characterized by cold temperatures and strong winds. Page 139.

board resolution: a formal decision or statement of opinion adopted by a *board,* also called *board of directors,* an official group of persons who direct or supervise some activity. Page 100.

Bodhi: in Buddhism, one who has attained intellectual and ethical perfection by human means. Page 133.

born: brought into existence; created. Page 24.

borne: endured or tolerated. Page 143.

born out of: brought into existence from; created or developed because of. Page 87.

botany: the science or study of plants, their life, structure, growth, classification, etc. Page 24.

bow down: bend the head or the body or the knee as an expression of reverence or submission. Also used figuratively. Page 19.

Bowie, Jim: (1796–1836) American pioneer who fought for Texas independence from Mexico and was killed during the fighting at the *Alamo,* a mission and fort in San Antonio, Texas. Mexican troops attacked the Alamo on 23 February 1836, but the Americans held out until, ammunition running low, the fort was overrun on 6 March. Bowie and the other defenders were all killed, but the cry "Remember the Alamo!" served to rally additional forces to the cause of Texas independence, which was finally gained in April 1836. Page 106.

brawn: muscular strength, as opposed to intellectual power, such as that used in manual labor or physical work. Page 139.

breaks down: ceases to function. Page 132.

Bremerton: a city in west Washington, a state in the northwest United States on the Pacific coast. Page 10.

brickbat(s): literally, a piece of broken brick thrown as a weapon. Figuratively, a *brickbat* is an uncomplimentary remark, especially an insult or criticism. Page 147.

Bridge, the: the route to Clear and beyond, also referred to as *The Bridge to Total Freedom*. In Scientology, there is the idea of a bridge across the chasm. It comes from an old mystic idea of a chasm between where one is now and a higher plateau of existence, and that many people trying to make it fell into the abyss. Today, Scientology has a bridge which spans the chasm and brings one to a higher plateau. It is an exact route with precise procedures providing uniformly predictable spiritual gains when correctly applied. The Bridge is complete and can be walked with certainty. Page 2.

British Columbia: a province in western Canada on the Pacific coast, including Vancouver Island and the Queen Charlotte Islands. Page 31.

British Commonwealth: an association of countries, including England, Wales, Scotland, Northern Ireland and various self-governing states (such as Canada, Australia, New Zealand) that were formerly part of the British Empire. The Commonwealth was formally established in 1931 to encourage trade and friendly relations. Page 101.

brooding: preoccupied with depressing or painful memories or thoughts; worried or troubled. Page 141.

Browning: Robert Browning (1812–1889), English poet, noted for his finely drawn character studies in a style of poetry he developed called *dramatic monologues* (*monologue* means one person speaking). In these poems Browning speaks in the voice of an imaginary or historical character at a dramatic moment in that person's life. Page 81.

Brown, Professor: Thomas Benjamin Brown (1892–1962), American physics teacher at George Washington University, Washington, DC, from 1920 to 1958. Chairman of the Physics Department for more than thirty years, he received recognition as a dedicated teacher in the field and wrote several textbooks on the subject. Page 81.

brute: someone viewed as strong, tough or the like. Page 60.

brute force: the application of predominantly physical effort to achieve a goal; great physical strength. Page 139.

Buddhists: those who follow the doctrines of *Buddhism,* the religion founded by Indian philosopher Gautama Siddhartha Buddha (ca. 563–483? B.C.). *See also* **Gautama.** Page 65.

bulldog, hangs to…like a: with an unrelenting, stubborn persistence, likened to that of a bulldog. A *bulldog* is a medium-sized, muscular dog with a large head, a large broad nose and a deep, broad and full chest. The bulldog's lower jaw projects, enabling the dog to take a grip that is difficult to break. Page 23.

bunk: a narrow bed built like a shelf into or against a wall, as in a ship's cabin. Page 11.

burgeoning: growing or increasing rapidly; expanding. Page 92.

by reason of: on account of; because of. Page 137.

byroad: a side road or a minor road. Used figuratively to mean a course of action, investigation, etc., that is minor or less important when compared to others. Page 75.

C

calumny: the making of false and malicious statements in an effort to injure someone's reputation. Page 140.

Camelback Mountain: a mountain located in Phoenix, Arizona, that rises to a height of 2,700 feet (823 meters) above sea level. The name *Camelback* is derived from its shape, which resembles the head and hump of a kneeling camel. Page 52.

Campbell, Jr., John W.: (1910–1971) American editor and writer who began writing science fiction while at college. In 1937 Campbell was appointed editor of the magazine *Astounding Stories,* later titled *Astounding Science Fiction* and then *Analog.* Under his editorship *Astounding* became a major influence in the development of science fiction and published stories by some of the most important writers of that time. Page 18.

Capella: Martianus Capella, fifth-century A.D. scholar who wrote on astronomy, mathematics and other fields. Page 20.

capital: wealth in whatever form, used or capable of being used to produce more wealth. Page 79.

capitalistic: of or relating to *capitalism,* the economic system in which one loans money that, by accumulating interest (profit), will support a person in leisure. It is the process of making money work for one rather than one doing the work himself. Page 130.

cast(ing) away: rejecting; discarding. Page 21.

catcalls: loud shouts or cries made to express disapproval. Page 149.

categorically: absolutely, certainly and unconditionally, with no room for doubt, question or contradiction. Page 53.

Catherine the Great: Catherine II (1729–1796), empress of Russia from 1762 to 1796. During her reign, Catherine built schools and hospitals, promoted education and extended Russian territory. Page 106.

causality: the ability to cause an effect or the action that causes an effect. Page 51.

cedar: the fragrant, durable wood of cedar trees, used for thousands of years in construction of furniture, buildings and ships. Page 17.

cell(s): the smallest structural unit of an organism that is capable of independent functioning. All plants and animals are made up materially of one or more cells that usually combine to form various tissues. For instance, the human body has more than 10 trillion cells. Page 9.

cellularly: in a way that is *cellular,* having to do with a cell. *See also* **cell(s).** Page 9.

censor: in Freudian theory, that restraining force which keeps undesirable and distasteful ideas, impulses and feelings in the unconscious of an individual. Page 37.

certificate(s): an award given to designate study and practice performed and skill attained. A certificate is not a degree, since it signalizes competence, whereas a degree ordinarily symbolizes merely time spent in theoretical study and gives no index of skill. Page 68.

chagrin: a feeling of annoyance or humiliation due to disappointment about something. Page 52.

Chaldean: the people of *Chaldea,* an ancient region in what is now southeastern Iraq that came to rule over all of Babylonia, an empire in southwest Asia that flourished between 2100 and 689 B.C. Chaldean rulers helped develop a wealthy and powerful civilization in Babylonia. Page 19.

chap: an informal term for a fellow; a man or boy. Page 85.

chaps in white coats: a reference to psychiatrists and their attendants, etc., who characteristically wear white coats. Page 106.

cheela: a follower and pupil of a *guru,* a Hindu spiritual teacher. Page 18.

China, prerevolutionary: a reference to China in the period from roughly 1928 until 1949. During this time the government was controlled by the Chinese *Nationalists,* the political party that had overturned the emperor (1911) and established China as a nation with elected leaders. After 1928, the Nationalists tried to block a revolution by the increasingly powerful Chinese Communists. A civil war eventually broke out. By 1949, with a Communist victory assured, the Nationalists moved to Taiwan, an island off the southeast coast of China, and set up a separate government. Page 75.

Christ: one of the world's greatest religious leaders. The Christian religion was founded on his life and teachings. Page 65.

Christian(s): a follower of the Christian religion based on the life and teachings of Jesus Christ. Most Christians believe God sent Jesus into the world as the Savior. Page 65.

Christophe: Henri Christophe (1767–1820), black king in northern Haiti in the early 1800s and one of Haiti's national heroes. In 1779, he and hundreds of other Haitians fought on the side of the Americans in the Revolutionary War in America. Following, he went to Haiti and led that revolution, throwing out the French and helping establish the independent country of Haiti in 1804. In 1806 he was named the president of Haiti. Page 80.

chrome: a glossy, fairly soft, gray metal. Chrome resists corrosion and becomes bright and shiny when polished. It is used to coat other metals, giving them a durable, shiny finish. It also hardens steel and is used for armor plate on ships, tanks and safes. Page 125.

Church of Christ: the common name for a group of churches, *Churches of Christ,* independent Christian congregations that purposefully have no overall formal organization and are associated with one another through their common faith in the Bible and adherence to its teachings. Page 52.

circle: a group of people bound together by common interests. Page 51.

circle, come full: return to an earlier or first position or situation after leaving it. Page 116.

circle, inner: a small group of people within a larger group, who have a lot of power, influence and special information. Page 147.

circuit, mental: an established pattern or series of thoughts or concerns, such as those relating to one's usual routines, likened to a regular journey around a specific area. Page 84.

circumventing: finding a way around (an obstacle). Page 40.

Citadel of a Christophe: also *Citadelle Laferrière,* a famous mountain fortress constructed on top of a 3,100-foot (1,000-meter) peak outside the city of Cap Haitien in Haiti. Built during the early 1800s by Haitian king Henri Christophe (1767–1820), it took thousands of slaves to construct the massive walls, which were many feet thick and between 100 to 200 feet (30.5 to 61 meters) high. The fortress was supposedly built to house fifteen thousand men with enough food and water to last for a year. Page 80.

clashes: conflicts, as between differing interests, views or purposes. Page 138.

Classification, Gradation and Awareness Chart: *Classification, Gradation and Awareness Chart of Levels and Certificates,* the route to Clear and OT (also called *The Bridge to Total Freedom,* or the *Bridge*). First released in 1965, it is the master program for every case. *Classification* refers to training and the fact that certain actions are required, or skills attained, before an individual is classified for a particular training level and allowed onto the next class. *Gradation* refers to the gradual improvement that occurs in Scientology auditing. *Awareness* refers to one's own awareness, which improves as one progresses up. Scientology contains the entire map for getting the individual through all the various points on this gradation scale, getting him across the Bridge and to a higher state of existence. Page 120.

Clear: the *Clear* is a person who is not aberrated. He is rational in that he forms the best possible solutions he can on the data he has and from his viewpoint. This is achieved through *clearing,* releasing all the physical pain and painful emotion from the life of an individual. See *Dianetics: The Modern Science of Mental Health.* Page 35.

climate: the most noticeable or most frequent attitudes, standards or environmental conditions of a group, period, place or thing. Page 80.

cloister: literally, a place where people live a life of religious seclusion and contemplation. Used figuratively for any place that is secluded or sheltered from the harsh realities of life. Page 2.

closed-circuit: of or relating to a *closed-circuit television system,* in which the signals are transmitted from one or more cameras by cable to a restricted group of monitors (television receiving sets), usually to view some special event taking place remote from the viewers. Page 150.

close hand, at: very nearby. Page 140.

clothed in: covered with, or as with, clothes. Used figuratively, indicating the spirit is covered by flesh (the human body) as though it were clothes. Page 125.

co-audit: auditing by a team of any two people who are auditing each other. Short for *cooperative auditing.* Page 44.

cognizant: fully aware of or having knowledge of something. Page 40.

come full circle: return to an earlier or first position or situation after leaving it. Page 116.

commencement: the beginning of something. Page 75.

Commonwealth, British: an association of countries, including England, Wales, Scotland, Northern Ireland and various self-governing states (such as Canada, Australia, New Zealand) that were formerly part of the British Empire. The Commonwealth was formally established in 1931 to encourage trade and friendly relations. Page 101.

Communications Course: a Scientology course that covers basic communications skills, through which one gains the ability to effectively communicate with others. Page 144.

communism: the political theory or system in which all property and wealth is owned by all the members of a classless society and a single party with absolute power runs the economic and political systems of the state. Extensive restrictions are enforced on personal and religious liberties and freedom, and individual rights are overruled by the collective needs of the masses. Page 14.

compendium: a collection of concise, but detailed, information that lays out the important features of a particular subject. Page 102.

compose: create a piece of music. Page 142.

conceit: an idea or opinion, especially one that is fanciful or unusual in some way. Page 80.

cone: any object or space having the shape of a *cone,* an object that has a broad circular base at one end and comes to a point at the top, or has a circular top and tapers to a point at the bottom. Page 11.

confound: to make feel confused; bewilder. Page 41.

Congressional Airport: an airport that was located near Washington, DC. It was the location of various flying schools and, in the early 1930s, was a site where LRH participated in stunt flying. Page 82.

conjured: called or brought into existence by, or as if by, magic (usually followed by *up*). Page 14.

consigned: assigned (something) to a particular category; classified (something) as belonging to a certain order of things. Page 83.

conspired: agreed together, especially secretly, to do something wrong, evil or illegal. Page 136.

Constantinople: a former name for Istanbul, the largest city in Turkey. Founded in 667 B.C., the city was made capital of the eastern part of the Roman Empire in A.D. 330. In the early days of Christianity, Constantinople held a key position in the Christian Church, comparable to that of Rome. Page 101.

contemplative: given to *contemplation*, the action of thinking about something profoundly and at length. Page 2.

contemporary: of the same time; existing or occurring at, or dating from, the same period of time as something or somebody else. Page 106.

contention: a statement or point that one argues for as true. Page 125.

context: the interrelated conditions in which something exists or occurs. Page 1.

contingent: a group of people representing a particular organization or belief, or from a particular region or country, and forming part of a larger group. Page 33.

conversants: those who know about something or are familiar with it, from experience or use. Page 21.

Copernican system: the astronomical theory that the Earth and other planets revolve around the Sun, a theory put forth by Polish astronomer Nicolaus Copernicus (1473–1543) in 1543. This theory challenged the system (favored since the second century), that held that the Sun and planets revolved around the Earth. Page 23.

Copernicus: Nicolaus Copernicus (1473–1543), Polish astronomer best known for his astronomical theory that the Earth and other planets revolve around the Sun. Published in 1543, this theory challenged the system (favored since the second century), which held that the Sun and planets revolved around the Earth. Page 20.

copier: *tape copying machine,* a machine that makes an exact copy of a tape, as in reproducing duplicates of an original recording. *See also* **recorder.** Page 92.

cornerstone: literally, a stone that forms the base of a corner of a building, joining two walls. Hence a fundamentally important basis on which things are constructed or developed. Page 1.

coroneresquely: in the manner of or as would be determined by a *coroner,* an official who is responsible for investigating the deaths of people who have died in a sudden, violent or unusual way. Page 85.

cortex: the outer layer of the brain, consisting of nerve cell bodies, folded into a surface with many grooves and ridges. The cortex is said to be responsible for the function of receiving and identifying sensations such as touch, sight and hearing, handling voluntary muscle movement of the body, memory, thought and reasoning. Page 132.

corvette: a lightly armed, fast ship used especially during World War II (1939–1945) to accompany a group of supply ships and protect them from attack by enemy submarines. Page 89.

cracking: finding and resolving the difficulties of; solving. Page 108.

creditable: worthy of belief. Page 61.

credulity: readiness or willingness to believe something, such as information, reports, etc. Page 138.

creed: any system of beliefs or principles in general. Page 2.

Cross, Scientology: the Scientology Cross is an eight-pointed cross representing the eight dynamics of life through which each individual is striving to survive: (1) self; (2) sex, the family and the future generation; (3) groups; (4) Mankind; (5) life, all organisms; (6) matter, energy, space and time—MEST—the physical universe; (7) spirits; and (8) the Supreme Being. In *Dianetics: The Modern Science of Mental Health* the first four dynamics are described, because Dianetics covers the first four dynamics. Scientology covers all eight dynamics. Page 3.

crucified: treated with gross injustice; persecuted; tormented; tortured. Page 21.

crux: the decisive or most important point of a problem, question or situation. Page 99.

cryptic: deliberately mysterious, or having a secret meaning. Page 18.

crystalline spheres: the revolving concentric transparent shells on which heavenly bodies were thought to be fixed as they moved around the Earth. Page 20.

cultured: produced under artificial and controlled conditions, such as plants, microorganisms or animal tissue that is grown in specially controlled conditions for scientific, medical or commercial purposes. Page 9.

cumulation: the action of heaping up, gathering or accumulating something; accumulation. Page 23.

cunning: inventive skill or imagination in doing something; cleverness. Page 149.

Curtain, slipping through the: *slipping* means moving or passing quietly, easily and quickly. A *curtain* is a piece of cloth or similar material that serves to cover or conceal what is behind it. Used here figuratively to refer to the unconsciousness of death. Page 11.

cut above, a: a step ahead of someone or something; higher in rank or quality; superior. The word *cut* as used here refers to a step or degree of something, such as in an economic or social scale or the like; *above* means in, at or to a higher place. Page 120.

cytological: of, relating to or by the methods of cytology. *See also* **cytology**. Page 9.

cytology: the branch of biology dealing with the structure, function and life history of cells. Page 22.

D

damnation: condemnation to Hell or eternal punishment. Page 101.

Dark Ages: the period in European history from the A.D. 400s to the 1000s. The term refers to the intellectual darkness, such as lack of learning and schooling during this period, the loss of many artistic and technical skills, and the virtual disappearance of the knowledge of the previous Greek and Roman civilizations. Page 125.

Darwin: Charles Darwin (1809–1882), English naturalist and author. His book *On the Origin of Species* proposed a theory to explain evolution of life forms to higher forms. Page 9.

Darwinian theory: a reference to the theory of evolution of English naturalist and author Charles Darwin (1809–1882) that Man descended and evolved from the lower life forms to what he is today. This theory holds that all species of plants and animals developed from earlier forms and that the forms that are best adapted to their environment survive and reproduce, while those that are less well adapted die out. According to popular belief, the theory of evolution stated that Man descended from monkeys. Page 9.

dawn: the beginning or rise of anything. Page 1.

dead mathematics: *dead* means no longer current or in practice. *Mathematics* means the study of the relationships among numbers, shapes and quantities, using numbers and symbols. *Dead mathematics* refers to a mathematics that is no longer of any use. Page 139.

decisive: that settles or can settle a dispute, question, etc.; conclusive. Page 92.

decry: speak out against strongly and openly; denounce. Page 21.

definitive: having a fixed and final form; providing a solution or final answer; satisfying all requirements. Page 10.

degradation: a way of life without dignity, health or any social comforts; a condition of extreme poverty and uncaring neglect. Page 149.

deliver: 1. present or give, used here in reference to the Gnostic belief that part of each person was divine and that this part was imprisoned in the body (matter). The divine part would have to live in the material world until it had been cleansed of matter and had reached full spiritual knowledge, at which point it would arrive (be delivered) into the presence of God. *See also* **Gnostic**. Page 51.

2. state or present. Page 51.

3. provide something to another. Page 52.

deluge myth: the story of a massive flood that covered the Earth thousands of years ago. The flood destroyed all living things except those that God permitted to survive. Similar stories are found in the religious traditions of many peoples, including Native Americans, peoples of the Middle East and southern Asia and others. Page 31.

Democritus: (460–370 B.C.) Greek philosopher who developed the atomic theory of the universe, which had been originated by his teacher, the philosopher Leucippus. According to Democritus, all things are composed of minute, invisible, indestructible particles of pure matter that move about eternally in infinite empty space. Democritus believed that our world came about from the chance combination of atoms. Page 22.

demystification: removal of the mystery surrounding something; clarification. Page 99.

denomination: a religious group united under a common faith with a specific name and organization. Page 67.

denounced: criticized harshly. Page 144.

depression: 1. a period marked by slackening of business activity, increased unemployment, falling prices and wages, etc., particularly the economic crisis and period of low business activity in the United States and other countries, roughly beginning with the stock market crash in October 1929 and continuing through most of the 1930s. Page 89.

2. a feeling of sadness in which a person feels there is no hope for the future. Page 148.

deranged: disturbed mentally; insane. Literally, put out of order, disordered, disarranged. Page 36.

desolate: deprived of hope, joy or comfort, like one deserted by friends or relatives; miserable. Page 155.

desolation: a feeling of loneliness, abandonment, sorrow, hopelessness and despair. Page 149.

detached: separated or disconnected. Page 90.

devil would fear to tread, where the: a variation of the saying *Fools rush in where angels fear to tread,* meaning people with little experience or knowledge often get involved in difficult situations that those with superior wisdom and understanding avoid. This expression comes from a line in the poem *An Essay on Criticism* (1711) by English poet Alexander Pope (1688–1744), where he discusses the laws by which a critic should be guided and gives examples of critics who have violated these laws. By extension, a place *"where the devil would fear to tread"* is a place so dangerous that even a devil would not want to go there. Page 25.

Dharma: the name of a legendary Hindu sage and of a body of scientific philosophical-religious truths, written around 600 B.C. The Dharma rose up in Asia and its doctrines were spread to hundreds of millions of people by the founder of Buddhism, Siddhartha Gautama Buddha (ca. 563–483? B.C.). Page 65.

Dhyana: in Buddhism and Hinduism, spiritual enlightenment that is achieved through higher states of contemplation. Page 65.

diabolical: extreme or exceedingly great in degree. Page 41.

dialectic: originally the practice of attempting to arrive at the truth by the exchange of logical arguments or back-and-forth questions and answers. Later the word was used to describe the theory that the evolution of ideas occurs because a concept gives rise to its opposite, thus creating a conflict, the result of which is a third view, supposedly at a higher level of truth than the first two views. German revolutionist Karl Marx (1818–1883) altered this, viewing life as material only and containing contradictory sides or aspects ("struggle of opposites"), the conflicts of which are the driving forces of change and result in development and the emergence of something new. Page 80.

dialectic materialism: a theory adopted as the official philosophy of communism, based on the works of German revolutionist Karl Marx (1818–1883). The theory maintains that the material world has reality independent of the mind or spirit and ideas can arise only from material conditions. Marx asserted that everything is material, including human culture. He stated all things naturally contain contradictory sides or aspects ("struggle of opposites"), the conflicts of which are the driving forces of change and result in development and the emergence of something new. Page 79.

Dianetics: Dianetics is a forerunner and substudy of Scientology. Dianetics means "through the mind" or "through the soul" (from Greek *dia*, through, and *nous*, mind or soul). It is a system of coordinated axioms which resolve problems concerning human behavior and psychosomatic illnesses. It combines a workable technique and a thoroughly validated method for increasing sanity, by erasing unwanted sensations and unpleasant emotions. Page 1.

Dianetics Symbol: the Dianetics Symbol uses the triangular shape of the Greek letter *delta* as its basic form. It is made up of stripes of green (which stands for growth) and stripes of yellow (which stands for life). The four green stripes represent the four dynamics of Dianetics: survival as (I) self, (II) sex and family, (III) group and (IV) Mankind. Page 2.

diaphragm: a wide muscular partition between the lungs and the stomach, which tightens when one inhales and relaxes when one exhales. Page 88.

diatribe: a forceful and bitter verbal attack. Page 23.

dictum: a short statement that expresses a general truth or principle. Page 117.

directorship: a position as a director (one of a group of persons chosen to control or govern the affairs of an organization), especially on a board of directors. Page 137.

disabused: freed of a mistaken or misguided notion. Page 2.

discerned: perceived or recognized mentally; understood. Page 31.

discourse(s): serious conversation or discussion about something. Page 2.

discredit: cause people to stop believing in (someone or something). Page 52.

discreditable: damaging to (someone's) reputation or status; disgraceful. Page 142.

disintegration: a process causing the breakup of an atomic nucleus or of a particle within an atom into smaller parts, either by radioactive decay or through bombardment with high-energy particles. Page 24.

dismal: depressingly gloomy or cheerless. Page 136.

dispatched: sent off promptly to a destination. Page 108.

dissipated: caused to diminish, fade or vanish. Page 13.

distilled: derived from, or expressed in a summarized form, a wider experience or larger set of ideas. Page 33.

Doctor of Divinity: an ordained minister of the Church of Scientology permitted to marry, bury and baptize parishioners and to hold confessionals. Page 67.

doggone: an exclamation used to express irritation, anger, disgust, etc. Page 60.

dogma: a belief or set of beliefs that a religion holds to be true. Page 52.

done away with: gotten rid of; put an end to. Page 143.

downs: treeless, hilly areas with fairly smooth slopes usually covered with grass, particularly as found in southern England. Page 116.

drawing pen: an instrument that varies the width of strokes according to how much pressure the user applies. Page 116.

driftwood: broken pieces of wood that are found washed up on a beach or floating on a body of water. Page 44.

drudge: a person who does distasteful or dull work, or who works in a routine, unimaginative way. Page 21.

dubbed: gave a descriptive name to something; called. Page 42.

dubbed-in: added, inserted or placed along with something else. *Dub-in* is a term used to characterize vision or recall which is imaginary. The term comes from the motion picture industry. To "dub," in moviemaking, is to create and add sounds to a picture after filming is complete. This process ("dubbing") results in a fabricated soundtrack that seems to the audience like it actually took place when filmed, but much or all of it was created in the studio long after filming was finished and then "dubbed in." Page 106.

Durant, Will: William (Will) James Durant (1885–1981), American author, historian and popularizer of philosophy. Durant's book *The Story of Philosophy* (1926) explains in simple language the central ideas of the world's greatest philosophers and tells of their lives. Despite criticism from many critics and scholars who condemned the book for its simplified style, easily comprehensible to the average reader, *The Story of Philosophy* was immensely popular, selling millions of copies in a dozen languages. Page 147.

dwell on: spend (much) time upon or linger over (a thing) in action or thought; remain with the attention fixed on. Page 122.

dynamic: 1. from the Greek *dunamikos,* powerful. Hence, motivating or energizing force (of existence or life), as in *Dynamic Principle of Existence.* Page 36.
2. involving or relating to energy and forces that produce motion. Page 77.

Dynamic Principle of Existence: the lowest common denominator of existence—the discovery by L. Ron Hubbard that the goal of life can be considered to be infinite survival. Man, as a life form, can be demonstrated to obey in all his actions and purposes the one command, *"Survive!"* It is not a new thought that Man is surviving. It is a new thought that Man is motivated only by survival. Page 36.

E

easy, taking it: working or doing something in a relaxed way. Page 106.

echelon: a level, as in a steplike arrangement or order. An *echelon* is one of a series in a field of activity. Page 35.

ecumenical: relating to, involving or promoting the unity of Christian Churches around the world. Page 101.

1870: the time period during which modern psychology was formulated, from the work of Wilhelm Wundt (1832–1920), German psychologist and physiologist (specialist in the study of the functions of physical, living things and the ways in which their parts and organs work). His work pushed a physiological basis for psychology and the false doctrine that Man is no more than an animal. Page 119.

electron: a tiny particle of matter that is far smaller than an atom and has a negative electrical charge. Electrons form a part of all atoms and are thought to rotate around the center of the atom. Page 23.

electronics: the science dealing with the design, development and application of devices and systems involving the flow of electrical energy, such as radio, television, computers, rockets, etc. Page 125.

Elizabeth, New Jersey: a city in northeastern New Jersey, USA, which was the location of the first Hubbard Dianetic Research Foundation, 1950–1951. Page 31.

elucidates: makes clear, explains. Page 41.

emanation(s): something that flows out, as from a source or origin. Page 68.

embraces: includes as part of a broader whole; contains. Page 1.

embryo: the unborn young of a human in the earliest stages of development, specifically from conception to about the eighth week. Page 42.

Empedocles: (490?–430 B.C.) Greek philosopher, statesman and poet. He asserted that all things are composed of the four basic elements: earth, air, fire and water. His view of evolution was that humans and animals evolved from earlier forms. Page 22.

empirically: in a way that is based on or characterized by observation and experiment rather than theory. Page 52.

encapsulated: expressed in concise, summarized form, as if from being placed in a *capsule,* a small case or container. Page 136.

encroaching: intruding gradually or stealthily, often taking away somebody's authority, rights or property. Page 52.

endeavor(s): a serious, determined effort. Page 14.

endocrine system: a system of glands that secrete hormones (chemical substances) from certain organs and tissues in the body. These glands and their hormones regulate the growth, development and function of certain tissues and coordinate many processes within the body. Page 33.

endocrinological: of or having to do with *endocrinology,* the branch of biology dealing with the endocrine system. *See also* **endocrine system.** Page 33.

endowed: given money or property so as to provide an income or support. Page 24.

end sheet(s): a sturdy sheet of paper, often distinctively colored or ornamented, pasted to the inside of a book's front or back cover and to the inside (spine) edge of the first or last page. Page 35.

engram bank: the storage place in the body where engrams, with all their percepts, are recorded and retained and from which engrams act upon the analytical mind and the body. By *percepts* is meant impressions or mental results of perceiving by the senses; things that are perceived. Page 39.

engulfed: overwhelmed (something) with a great amount of something (such as superstition). Page 125.

enigma: something that is not easily understood; a puzzling or unexplainable situation, event or occurrence. Page 55.

ensue: follow as a consequence or result. Page 61.

entangling: involving in something confused or complicated. Page 90.

enthralling: intensely interesting; thrilling. Page 117.

epigram: a concise, witty remark or saying, often with a clever twist in thought. Page 21.

equated: put in the form of an equation. Page 36.

equation: 1. a mathematics term showing that two things are of the same value or equal each other. For example, 3x = 9 means that 3 times x is equal to 9. (From this equation one calculates that x = 3.) Page 22.

2. a situation that has a number of variable elements to be considered. Page 36.

erased: of an engram, caused to "vanish" entirely by recountings, at which time it is filed as memory and experience. Page 40.

Eratosthenes: (276?–195? B.C.) Greek geographer, astronomer and mathematician. Page 20.

essence: something that exists, especially that which is spiritual or immaterial. Page 18.

essence, in the final: most basically or fundamentally. Page 63.

et al.: abbreviation for the Latin phrase *et alia*, meaning "and others." Page 77.

eternal: without beginning or end; lasting forever; always existing. Page 101.

ethnology: the science that analyzes cultures, especially in regard to their historical development and the similarities and dissimilarities between them. Page 75.

Euclid: (ca. 300 B.C.) Greek mathematician whose chief work, *Elements* (a comprehensive set of thirteen volumes covering geometry, the theory of numbers and other related subjects), was used as a standard instructional text for 2,000 years. A modified version of the first few volumes still forms the basis for instruction in certain fields of mathematics. Page 125.

evangelist: a person who seeks to convert others to the Christian faith, especially by public preaching. Page 52.

exactitude: the quality of being *exact*, accurate and correct in all important details. Page 13.

exact science(s): any of the sciences, such as physics and chemistry, that study and analyze the nature and properties of energy and nonliving matter. *Exact* refers to the methods and procedures used in such sciences and means requiring accuracy and precision; not involving vagueness or uncertainty. Page 19.

exalted: marked by nobility of thought; of an exceedingly high character. Page 51.

exhaustive: leaving no part unexamined or unconsidered; complete; thorough. Page 31.

expansive: having a wide range or extent; comprehensive; extensive. Page 51.

Explorers Club: an organization, headquartered in New York and founded in 1904, devoted exclusively to promoting the science of exploration. To further this aim, it provides grants for those who wish to participate in field research projects and expeditions. It has provided logistical support for some of the twentieth century's most daring expeditions. L. Ron Hubbard was a lifetime member of the Explorers Club. Page 139.

expunging: getting rid of something completely, doing away with. Page 101.

exteriorization: the act of becoming exterior to the body. Page 123.

extrapolated: used known facts as the starting point from which to draw conclusions about something unknown. Page 31.

eyelids, heavied the: made the eyelids have difficulty in staying open, as if seeming to feel heavy from drowsiness or sleepiness. Page 83.

F

face of, in the: when confronted with. Page 2.

facetious: lacking serious intent; not meant to be taken seriously. Page 22.

far-flung: extended far or to a great distance; remote. Page 108.

fascistic: of or relating to *fascism,* a governmental system led by a dictator having complete power, which forcibly suppresses opposition and criticism, and regiments all industry, commerce, etc. Page 130.

fateful: having far-reaching consequences or implications; critically important. Page 52.

feature(s): a part of something that is especially prominent and that distinguishes it from other things. Page 9.

fell charge, one: a variation of *one fell swoop,* all at one time or at the same time; in one sudden action or stroke, as of a bird of prey (a bird such as an eagle or hawk that kills and eats small animals) making one vigorous descent upon its victim. The word *fell* in this expression means vigorous. Page 80.

fetus: the unborn human in the womb, from after the second month of pregnancy until birth. Page 41.

field: a sphere of activity, interest, action or operation, etc. Page 7.

fire: hurl or direct with force and suddenness. Page 23.

firestorm: an intense outpouring or outburst. Page 33.

First Principles: a book by English philosopher Herbert Spencer (1820–1903), originally planned as the first part of his multivolume work *A System of Synthetic Philosophy.* In *First Principles,* published in 1862, Spencer presents his basic views on philosophy and knowledge, with examples from many fields. *See also* **Spencer, Herbert** and ***Synthetic Philosophy.*** Page 21.

floored: stunned or astounded. Page 88.

flown: passed with speed. Page 26.

flutterings: rapid beatings, as in the heart. Page 41.

folkloric: based on or resembling *folklore,* the traditional beliefs, legends, sayings, customs, etc., of a culture. Page 75.

folly: foolishness. Page 141.

footnote: a comment or remark added to a main statement. Page 52.

forbidding: unfriendly or threatening in appearance. Page 149.

forebears: those living at an earlier time and from whom a person, family or group has descended; ancestors. Page 62.

forego: do without the enjoyment or advantage of; give up. Page 137.

foreshadow: an indication of something beforehand; an indication of what is to come. Page 123.

forging: forming or making by concentrated effort. From the literal meaning of *forge*, form by heating and hammering; beat into shape. Page 152.

formidable: causing fear, dread or anxiety. Page 76.

formulated: expressed in precise form; stated definitely or systematically. Page 36.

forty-below: of a temperature that is extremely cold. In the Fahrenheit scale of temperature, thirty-two degrees above zero is freezing. Thus a temperature of forty degrees below zero, more than seventy degrees below the point of freezing, is extremely cold. Page 139.

Foundation(s): any of the early Hubbard Dianetic Research Foundations that were located throughout the United States and which trained students in Dianetics. Page 90.

Founding Church: the Founding Church of Scientology, Washington, DC, established in 1955. A *founding church* is one from which other churches have their origin or derive their authority. Page 76.

fraternity: a society of college or university students and graduates, most of which form their names from two or three letters of the Greek alphabet. Page 82.

Freud, Sigmund: (1856–1939) Austrian founder of psychoanalysis who emphasized that unconscious memories of a sexual nature control a person's behavior. Page 75.

frontier: the land or territory that forms the furthest extent of settled or inhabited regions. Used literally and figuratively. Page 22.

frontiersman: a man living on a frontier, especially in a newly pioneered territory of the United States. In early US history, frontiersmen were vital in the conquest of the land. Page 106.

frowned upon: viewed with disapproval. Page 139.

fruition: attainment of something desired or worked for; accomplishment. Page 26.

F Street: a street in Washington, DC, near the White House, location of George Washington University. Page 82.

fundamentalist: of *fundamentalism*, a conservative movement among Protestants in the United States that began in the late nineteenth century. It strongly objected to attempts to reconcile traditional Christian beliefs and doctrines with contemporary experience and knowledge, as well as to acceptance of a scientific view of the world. Page 52.

G

Gamow, George: (1904–1968) Russian-born American physicist who conducted research in nuclear physics while on the faculty of George Washington University. He played a key role in launching the project to develop atomic bombs for the United States during World War II (1939–1945). Page 81.

Gautama: Gautama Siddhartha Buddha (ca. 563–483? B.C.), Indian philosopher and the founder of *Buddhism,* one of the world's great religions. *Buddha* means "Enlightened One." After experiencing enlightenment for himself, Buddha sought to find release from the suffering of life for other people so they could achieve a state of complete happiness and peace. To achieve this, people had to free themselves of all desires and material things. Page 65.

George Washington University: a private university, founded in 1821, in the city of Washington, DC. Named after the first president of the United States, George Washington (1732–1799), it maintains various schools of education, including the School of Engineering and Applied Science and the Columbian College of Arts and Sciences. The university has a long history of supporting research in physics and other technical fields. Page 75.

given rise to: originated; produced; caused. Page 1.

glandular: of or relating to the glands (cells, groups of cells or organs in the body producing a secretion). For example, adrenal glands produce *adrenaline,* a hormone that is released into the bloodstream in response to physical or mental stress, as from fear of injury. It initiates many bodily responses, including stimulation of heart action and increase in blood pressure. Page 89.

gloomy: having a lot of sadness or hopelessness. Page 141.

Gnostic: of or relating to *Gnosticism,* a religious philosophy among early Christians who believed in salvation through *gnosis,* special knowledge of spiritual mysteries. The Gnostics explained the world as being made of two opposed aspects, good and evil. Each person was a combination of spirit, which was good, and matter, which was evil. The philosophy encouraged rejection of the material world so that the spirit could attain gnosis and be reunited once more with God. Page 51.

golden dawn: the beginning or rise of great happiness and achievement. Page 51.

good old days: an expression used when referring to a former time, remembered with nostalgia, as being better than the present, and sometimes despite modern improvements in science, technology, etc. Page 59.

Gordian knot, slashed (the): solved a virtually impossible or seemingly unsolvable problem. The phrase originates from the knot tied by King Gordius of Phrygia (an ancient country in what is now central Turkey), which legends said would be undone by one who was to rule Asia. Alexander the Great (356–323 B.C.) slashed through the knot with his sword and went on to subdue Greece, Egypt and central Asia as far as east India. Page 19.

"Gott Mit Uns": a German phrase meaning "God with us," a motto that was on the uniform belt buckles of German soldiers during World War I (1914–1918) and World War II (1939–1945). Page 129.

governor: an appointed or elected official who governs an area such as a colony, province or the like for a specified term. Page 141.

grace: elegance or beauty of form, manner, motion or action. Page 60.

grace of God, beyond the: beyond or outside the reaches of the love, favor or goodwill shown by God. Page 101.

gracing: adding elegance, beauty or charm to something. Page 61.

Grade VA: an intermediate step just above Grade V (Power). Grade VA, Power Plus, consists of added Power Processes. Handling Grade VA reduces parts of the whole track and permits the recovery of knowledge. Page 123.

gradient: moving or changing gradually, in steps or stages. Page 106.

grandly: in a grand (impressive, magnificent, etc.) manner. Page 19.

grave: very serious. Page 99.

gravitically: in a way that is related to a force or an attraction, as toward an object or point of influence, likened to *gravity,* the physical force by which bodies tend to move toward the center of the Earth. Page 22.

grim: depressing or worrying to consider. Page 2.

H

habitable: suitable or good enough to live in. Page 61.

hack: figuratively, get something done by breaking through blocks or obstructions. From the literal meaning of *hack,* clear (a road, path, etc.) by cutting away vines, trees, brush or the like. Page 116.

hairline: a very thin line. Page 150.

hallowed: regarded with great respect or reverence. Page 52.

halls of learning: buildings used by a college or university for teaching or research. Page 147.

harken back: refer back, as in coming from an earlier source. Page 18.

Harvey, William: (1578–1657) English physician who, using scientific procedures and experimentation, discovered that blood circulates and that the heart propels it through the body, thus refuting earlier theories. Page 37.

heady: exciting; exhilarating. Page 18.

heavied the eyelids: made the eyelids have difficulty in staying open, as if seeming to feel heavy from drowsiness or sleepiness. Page 83.

heavy weather: a figurative phrase meaning troubles, obstacles, difficulties, etc., that arise. Literally *heavy* here means overcast and dark skies, perhaps with rain, gloomy clouds, etc. It can also refer to the turbulence, great force or intensity of high waves at sea that may make the normal operations on a ship very difficult. Thus, if one is facing trouble, obstacles, difficulties, etc., he could figuratively be said to be in "heavy weather." Page 149.

hectically: with frantic and constant activity; in a hurried or frantic manner, as though things are barely under control. Page 61.

held office: occupied a position as an official or executive. Page 137.

held to: also *held up to,* shown or displayed for a specific reason, as in *"held (up) to ridicule,"* displayed as something to be made fun of. Page 19.

helmed: figuratively, held the position of leadership or control in an organization or endeavor; steered or directed. From the meaning of *helm* as used on a ship, the wheel by which the ship is steered. Page 92.

helter-skelter: in disorderly haste or confusion. Page 11.

hemlock: a poisonous drink made from *hemlock,* a plant of the parsley family that has purple-spotted stems and small white flowers. Greek philosopher Socrates was accused and convicted of corrupting the youth of Athens with unconventional ideas. When he was sentenced to death, he refused efforts to save his life and died after drinking a cup of poison hemlock given to him. *See also* **Socrates.** Page 144.

Heraclitus: (540?–480? B.C.) Greek philosopher who believed that fire is the original source of matter and that the entire world is in a constant state of change. Page 125.

Hereafter: a future life; a life or existence after death. Page 129.

Hermitage House: a publishing firm in New York City, New York, founded in 1947 by editor and publisher Arthur Ceppos (1910–1997). In May 1950, Hermitage House was the first to publish *Dianetics: The Modern Science of Mental Health.* Page 90.

hideous: shocking or horrible to the senses. Page 23.

Himalayas: a mountain range extending about 1,500 miles (2,400 kilometers) along the border between India and Tibet, containing some of the world's highest mountains, including Mount Everest. Page 120.

Hindu: 1. a native of India, especially one who follows the religion of *Hinduism,* a religion of India that emphasizes freedom from the material world through purification of desires and elimination of personal identity and which includes belief in reincarnation. Page 19.
2. also *Hindi,* one of the languages of India. Page 65.

hitherto: up to this time; until now. Page 33.

hold up (one's) head: to maintain (one's) dignity, self-respect or cheerfulness. Page 142.

Homer: a Greek poet of the ninth century B.C., best known for his writing of the epics, the *Iliad* and the *Odyssey*. The *Iliad* tells of Achilles, a Greek hero and soldier in the Trojan War. The *Odyssey* describes another Greek hero, Odysseus, while on his ten-year journey home, and the involvement of a number of Greek gods in his adventures. As a result of Homer's work, the Greeks formed many of their religious views from his portrayals of the gods and goddesses. Page 20.

horizon stars: stars as they rise and become visible on the horizon, used by early astronomers who would note the position of such stars and the time of their appearance. Page 23.

Hubbard Association of Scientologists (International): during the 1950s and 1960s, the organization that coordinated and provided guidance to all Scientology organizations over the world, served as the central point of dissemination and was the general membership group of the Church. Page 67.

Hubbard Communications Office: the Office of L. Ron Hubbard, originally organized with the purpose of handling and expediting the communication lines of LRH. The Hubbard Communications Office was later made one of the divisions of every Scientology organization and was assigned responsibility for building, holding, maintaining and manning the organization. Page 101.

hull, wheel and wing designs: the drawings that show how parts of an airplane are to be made, specifically the hull (the main body), the wheels and the wings. Page 24.

humanities: branches of learning (or, *humanity,* a branch of learning) concerned with human thought and relations, especially philosophy, literature, history, art, languages, etc., as distinguished from the natural sciences (sciences such as biology, chemistry and physics that deal with phenomena observable in nature); the social sciences including sociology (the science or study of the origin, development, organization and functioning of human society), psychology, economics, political science, etc. Originally, the *humanities* referred to education that would enable a person to freely think and judge for himself, as opposed to a narrow study of technical skills. Page 35.

humanity: the quality of being humane; kindness; benevolence. Page 149.

humming: in a busy state of activity. Page 23.

hybrid: characteristic of a *hybrid,* something of mixed origin or that is a mixture of different things. Page 25.

hypothesis: (plural *hypotheses*) a proposed explanation, set down as a starting point to provide a basis for further investigation, argument, etc. Page 23.

I

Ice Age: a period in Earth's history when ice covered a significant portion of the planet's surface and significant cooling of the atmosphere occurred. The *"last Ice Age"* refers to the most recent Ice Age, which ended 10,000 years ago. Page 31.

iconic: characteristic of an *icon,* something widely admired, especially when viewed as symbolizing a place, time period, culture or the like. Page 44.

ideology(ies): a system of ideas or way of thinking of a class or individual, especially as a basis of some economic or political theory or system. Page 56.

illumination: a spiritual or intellectual enlightenment, likened to supplying light to something. Page 115.

illusion: something that appears to exist or be a particular thing but does not actually exist or is in reality something else. Page 115.

illusive: having qualities of an *illusion,* as in being thought of as unreal, imaginary or the like. Page 11.

imagery: 1. visual images collectively. Page 44.
2. figurative description or illustration, used in literature to call up images in the mind. Page 115.

impala: a large, reddish-brown African antelope, with long curved horns, that makes spectacular leaps when alarmed. Page 80.

impassioned: filled with or expressing strong feelings. Page 144.

impeccably: in a way that conforms to the highest standards; perfectly. Page 94.

impenetrable: 1. not capable of being passed through. Page 41.
2. incapable of being understood. Page 147.

impetus, gave: provided the motivation or stimulus for. Page 105.

implicit: implied, rather than stated directly. Page 115.

import: the importance or significance of something. Page 141.

incontrovertible: not open to question or dispute; undeniable. Page 52.

incumbent upon: resting upon as a duty or obligation. Page 99.

indeterminate: not definite; not yet settled, concluded or known; inconclusive. Page 99.

indulgence(s): in Roman Catholicism, a freeing from all or part of the punishment for sins that have been forgiven, by Church authority. Such punishment (praying, fasting, etc.) is conceived needful since, even though the person is sorry for his sins and those sins have been forgiven, the consequences and weaknesses of sin remain with the person. In earlier times, the person could give money to pay for the indulgence rather than receive punishment. Page 101.

inexorably: in a manner impossible to stop or prevent; unalterably; inflexibly. Page 22.

Glossary 185

inexplicably: in a way that cannot be explained, understood or accounted for. Page 99.

infallible: something that is unfailing in effectiveness or is certain. Page 20.

infamy: very bad reputation; disgrace; dishonor. Page 141.

infers: implies or suggests something. Page 80.

inflation: a higher volume of money in circulation than there are goods, resulting in a continuing rise in the general price level. Page 130.

inherent(ly): existing in someone's or something's internal character as a permanent and inseparable element, quality or attribute. Page 9.

inner circle: a small group of people within a larger group, who have a lot of power, influence and special information. Page 147.

inorganic: not belonging to the body or its parts (such as its organs) or physical things. Page 35.

insignia: a symbol, badge or the like. The original insignia of Dianetics, which is the *Dianetics Symbol*, was designed in 1950. *See also* **Dianetics Symbol.** Page 35.

internal-combustion engine: an engine in which combustion occurs in a confined space called a *cylinder*. A mixture of fuel and air is fed into the cylinder, where its combustion creates high-pressure gases with rapid expansion. The suddenly expanding gases force a piston downwards in the cylinder, the movement of which transfers mechanical power to other parts of the engine or machinery. Page 24.

internment camps: prison camps for the confinement of enemy aliens (people who are not citizens of that country), prisoners of war, political prisoners, etc. Page 31.

in the face of: when confronted with. Page 2.

in the final essence: most basically or fundamentally. Page 63.

intrinsically: in a manner that belongs to something as one of the basic and essential elements that make it what it is. Page 2.

Ionian Greeks: those philosophers who lived and taught in the Greek colonies of Ionia, an ancient region on the west coast of Asia Minor (a historic region in west Asia now corresponding to part of Turkey) and on nearby islands in the Aegean Sea. The Ionian philosophers conceived the world to be made of physical elements (water, small particles of matter or the like), all controlled by a nonphysical guiding principle. Page 22.

iron horse: a slang term for a *locomotive,* an engine that pulls a railroad train. Page 26.

iron steed: a reference to a motorcycle. A *steed* is a horse, especially a high-spirited one. Page 60.

-isms: a distinctive belief, theory, system or practice, from words with the ending *-ism.* Page 79.

itinerant: being in one place for a comparatively short time and then moving on to another place. Page 52.

ivory tower: a place of retreat that is secluded and remote from the realities of the real world; some place or condition which is separated from everyday life. Page 89.

J

Janssen: a piano company founded in the early 1900s in New York City by Bernhard H. Janssen (1862–1933), who built a family business known for high-quality instruments. Page 68.

John Doe: a name given to an ordinary or typical person. Page 120.

Journal of Scientology: a magazine for Scientologists that was published twice monthly from 1952 to 1955. The *Journal of Scientology* carried technical articles, information of broad interest to members, general news and the like. Page 52.

Judah, Stillson: distinguished professor of religious history at the Pacific School of Religion, Berkeley, California, and Director of Libraries at the Graduate Theological Union, also in Berkeley. Dr. Judah was the author of several works on emerging religions. Page 3.

jump-off, point of: a place to start from, as of a journey, course of action, line of reasoning, etc. Page 88.

K

Kant: Immanuel Kant (1724–1804), German philosopher who maintained that objects of experience may be known but that things lying beyond the realm of possible experience (such as human freedom, the soul, immortality or God) are unknowable. This discouraged further investigation of the actual beingness and soul of Man. Page 22.

kingdom, animal: one of the three broad divisions of natural objects: the animal, vegetable and mineral kingdoms. A *kingdom* is a region or sphere of nature. Page 42.

kin, near of: a person's relative or relatives; from *kin*, meaning one's family. Page 85.

knowingness: the state or quality of knowing. In Scientology, it is a specialized term. Knowingness is not data. It is a feeling of certainty. It can be best defined by "knowing that one knows." True knowingness is a capability to know and to ascertain, within oneself, truth. Page 65.

Knowledge Cone, The: a chart that shows knowledge starting from a basic simplicity (at the top point of the cone) and branching out into greater and greater complexity as the cone widens toward the bottom. This bottom level includes fields and subjects, such as war, politics, etc., that are found in human societies and that Man tends to focus on, disregarding the higher and simpler truths in the cone. The chart further shows that this bottom level is a *worm's-eye view*, a close-up, but limited, view or grasp of things. Page 14.

Kodiak bear: a large brown bear inhabiting Kodiak Island (off the southwestern coast of Alaska) as well as coastal areas of Alaska and the west coast of Canada. Also called *Kodiak,* this bear can grow to a height of 9 feet (2.7 meters) and can attain a weight of around 1,700 pounds (780 kilograms). Page 140.

Koenig photometer: an early device that gave a visual representation of sound waves, invented by German physicist Karl Rudolf Koenig (1832–1901). A person would speak into a boxlike device which fed gas to a burner. The voice affected the flow of gas so that the ensuing flame flickered and varied in height proportionally to the sound waves. This was then reflected by a multisided spinning mirror (placed above the flame) into a bright band of light with distinctive dips and curves that corresponded to the sound impulses. Page 81.

L

lag: a period of time between one event and another event. Page 20.

laid to waste: completely destroyed or devastated (something). Page 77.

Lama: of *Lamaism,* a form of Buddhism practiced in Tibet and Mongolia. *See also* **lamaseries, Tibetan.** Page 90.

lamaseries, Tibetan: monasteries of *lamas,* priests or monks in *Lamaism,* a branch of Buddhism that seeks to find release from the suffering of life and attain a state of complete happiness and peace. Lamaism is practiced in Tibet, a land in south central Asia, and in areas such as Mongolia, a country to the north of China. Page 75.

landmark: marking a significant change or turning point in something, from *landmark,* an event, idea or item that represents a significant or historic development. Page 33.

Lao-tzu: (ca. sixth century B.C.) Chinese philosopher and founder of Taoism. According to legend, he wrote the *Tao Teh King* (The Classic of the Way and the Virtue), which had an enormous influence on Chinese thought and culture. It teaches that, because yielding (giving way to pressure or demands) eventually overcomes force, a wise man desires nothing. He never interferes with what happens naturally in the world or in himself. Page 65.

late: at a time period in or near the present time. Page 41.

lately: in a time period at or near the present time. Page 80.

latterly: at a subsequent time; later. Page 53.

lay: belonging to, pertaining to or performed by the people, as distinguished from the clergy. Page 67.

learned: 1. used to describe behavior or knowledge that is acquired through experience or training rather than being based on instincts. Page 9.
2. showing or characterized by deep or extensive knowledge. Page 13.

3. (of a person) having much knowledge acquired by study; highly educated. Page 23.

ledger, side of the: figurative reference to a *ledger,* a book with two sections or sides; information about income of funds is recorded on one side, and outgo on the other. Thus any of two opposing aspects, views or subjects could be referred to as one side or the other of a ledger. Page 22.

legend: the subject of a *legend,* stories and traditions about people or things that possess extraordinary qualities that are usually partly real and partly mythical. *Legend* also means a vast amount of persons or things. Page 120.

lens grinder: someone who grinds and polishes lenses to the correct curved shape, here used in reference to Dutch spectacle maker Hans Lippersheim (1570–1619), who is credited with inventing the first telescope in 1608. Though first used for military purposes, the telescope was soon after adapted by Italian physicist and astronomer Galileo Galilei (1564–1642), who used it to observe the Sun, Moon, planets and stars. Page 20.

liberal: not restricted to the exact or literal. Page 84.

Library of Congress: one of the largest libraries in the world, located in Washington, DC, and housing collections totalling more than 140 million items. It was established in 1800 by the US Congress (lawmaking body of the government) for service to its members but now also serves other government agencies, other libraries and the public. Page 88.

light of day, seen the: been brought forth or presented publicly. Page 89.

light of, in the: with the help given by knowledge of (some fact); taking into account; considering. Page 106.

line officer: a military or naval officer serving with combat units or warships, as distinguished from a supply officer, planning officer, advisor at headquarters, etc. Page 89.

literati: persons of scholarly or literary attainments; intellectuals. Page 33.

little people: people who are typical in having a small or average income and minimal power and influence; the common people, especially workers. Page 136.

localize: concentrate attention upon a particular thing or spot. Page 20.

locked: closed or held tightly inside; confined. Page 1.

lodestar(s): figuratively, a guiding star; that on which one's attention or hopes are fixed. A *lodestar* is one that shows the way, such as the North Star over the North Pole. Page 65.

lofty: elevated in character or spirit; figuratively, very high or tall. Page 125.

loggerheads, at: in disagreement or dispute. Page 136.

long since: in the distant past; long ago. Page 138.

loomed large: was regarded as significant, from the literal meaning of *loomed,* appeared, took shape or came in sight, especially in a large or important way. Page 115.

Los Angeles Daily News: a newspaper that was published in Los Angeles, California, from the early 1920s through the 1950s. The publication was originally named the *Daily Illustrated News*. Page 38.

lose its sting: remove the pain from a sting. Figuratively, *sting* means anything with the capacity or power to inflict mental pain or distress. Thus *"the threat of eternal damnation tended to lose its sting"* means it lost its power to produce pain or upset. Page 101.

Love Thy Neighbor: a reference to a widely known principle of conduct taught in many religions and societies, urging one to love those around one, including one's enemies. *Thy* is an older form of *your*. Page 130.

M

magic hand, wave a: a variation of *wave a magic wand*, used figuratively to mean produce wonderful appearances or results in one's environment, like the magical effects thought of as produced by a magician and coming from supernatural causes. A *magic wand* is literally a small, thin stick used in performing magic. Page 60.

mainline: principal or important. From the literal sense of *main line*, the principal line or route, as of a railroad. Page 115.

Man: the human race or species; humankind; Mankind. Page 2.

Manchuria: a region of northeastern China. Manchuria was invaded by the Japanese in 1931 and was held by Japanese forces until 1945, at the end of World War II (1939–1945). Page 75.

mandolin: a stringed musical instrument with a pear-shaped body and four or more pairs of strings. Page 138.

man in the street: the ordinary person, especially someone without specialized knowledge of the field in question. Page 147.

marionette: a puppet manipulated from above by strings attached to its jointed limbs. Page 38.

masses: ordinary people in society as a whole. Page 20.

materialism: in philosophy, the theory that physical matter is the only reality and that everything, including thought, feeling, mind and will, can be explained in terms of matter and physical phenomena. Page 79.

materialist: also *materialistic*, of or relating to materialism. *See also* **materialism.** Page 2.

materiality: material things; that which is material (formed or consisting of matter; physical); the physical world rather than the mind or spirit. Page 149.

material science(s): any of the sciences, such as physics and chemistry, that study and analyze the nature and properties of energy and nonliving matter. *Material* means of or pertaining to matter; physical. Page 124.

maze: 1. a device, consisting of a correct path concealed by blind alleys, used by people who study human and animal intelligence and learning. Page 76.
2. any complex system or arrangement that causes bewilderment or confusion. Page 117.

measuring stick: something against which one measures or judges value, worth, condition, etc. A *measuring stick* is an instrument, as a graduated rod, having a sequence of marks at regular intervals, which is used as a reference in determining length, height, etc. Used figuratively. Page 7.

mechanism(s): a structure or system (of parts, components, etc.) that together perform a particular function as would occur in a machine, as in *"gazes for the first time upon the mechanisms of human action"* or *"a man contained a mechanism which recorded with diabolical accuracy."* Page 41.

mechanistic: of or pertaining to a mechanism. *See also* **mechanism(s)**. Page 39.

memory: anything which, perceived, is filed in the standard memory bank and can be recalled by the analytical mind. Page 37.

mensurable: capable of being measured. Page 80.

mental image picture(s): a picture which is a complete recording, down to the last accurate detail, of every perception present in a moment of pain and partial or full unconsciousness. These mental image pictures have their own force and are capable of commanding the body. Page 90.

merger: blending, combining or joining of something with something else. Page 52.

mesmerized: completely captured the attention of; fascinated. Page 117.

metaphor: a word or phrase that ordinarily designates one thing used to designate another so as to make a comparison, as in "a sea of troubles" or "All the world's a stage." Page 115.

metaphysics: the branch of philosophy concerned with the ultimate nature of existence or the nature of ultimate reality that is above or goes beyond the laws of nature or is more than physical. First applied to writings of Aristotle (384–322 B.C.), the term literally means "after physics," as these writings followed his works entitled *The Physics*. Page 20.

methodical: done in a careful, logical and orderly way. Page 1.

meticulously: with extreme care about the smallest details; precisely. Page 47.

Michigan: a state in the north central United States. Page 100.

mildewed: decayed from age or disuse, as if covered with *mildew,* a gray or white fungus that grows on paper, fabrics, leather or other materials in damp conditions. Page 1.

milestone(d): furnished with *milestones,* stones set up beside a road to mark the distance to a particular place. Used figuratively to mean well traveled. Page 21.

ministers of state: heads of departments of a government. A *minister* is one who is appointed to head an executive or administrative department of the government. *State* means the government of a country. Page 106.

ministry(ies): the service, functions or profession of a minister of religion. Page 52.

mired: involved in difficulties that are hard to escape from; entangled. Literally, a *mire* is wet, slimy soil of some depth, or deep mud. Page 120.

mob: crowd around noisily, as from hostility. Page 140.

molds: becomes covered with or affected by mold (a growth of a type of fungus that causes matter to decay). Used figuratively to express that something becomes old, stale, neglected or out-of-date. Page 23.

monopoly: the exclusive possession or control of something. Page 143.

Monroe School: a public school located in Phoenix, Arizona. During late 1954 and early 1955, L. Ron Hubbard delivered weekly introductory lectures to the general public in the school's auditorium. Page 53.

Montana: a state in the northwestern United States bordering on Canada, where L. Ron Hubbard lived as a young boy. Page 75.

morass: something that traps, confuses or impedes; a state of confusion or entanglement. Page 14.

Moses: the principal leader and teacher of the Israelites and one of the most important characters in the Bible. He led his people out of slavery in Egypt to find their homeland in Palestine. At Mount Sinai (in Egypt) Moses declared the Ten Commandments as the law for his people. There the Israelites were established as a nation under his leadership. Page 65.

motor: of, pertaining to or involving muscular movement. Page 38.

mousetrap: a superior service or product. This phrase comes from a statement attributed to American lecturer, essayist and poet Ralph Waldo Emerson (1803–1882): "If a man can write a better book, preach a better sermon, or make a better mousetrap than his neighbor, though he builds his house in the woods the world will make a beaten path to his door." Page 90.

mud turtle: a freshwater turtle that lives at the bottom of muddy ponds and streams. Page 19.

Murphy, Bridey: a previous-life identity of Mrs. Virginia Tighe, an American born in 1923. In 1952, Tighe was the subject of amateur hypnotist Morey Bernstein. While under hypnosis, she began to relate detailed descriptions of people, places and things associated with a previous-life identity known as *Bridey Murphy,* born 20 December 1798, in Ireland. She used terms that were correct for the time and place and thus gave support to the validity of this identity. The details of her hypnotic sessions were recorded and published in a book entitled *The Search for Bridey Murphy*. It instantly became a bestseller and the story sparked a craze of reincarnation parties, magazine articles, songs about Bridey Murphy and even a movie. Page 105.

myelin sheathing: a whitish material that surrounds some nerve cells and that aids transmission of nerve impulses. Prior to 1950, prevailing theory held that the human child was incapable of recording memory until the formation of myelin sheathing after birth. Page 41.

mysticism: the belief that personal communication or union with truth or the divine (God, gods or goddesses) is achieved through direct perception or sudden insight rather than through rational thought. Page 36.

mythology: a body of myths, as that of a particular people or that relating to a particular person. A *myth* is a traditional story of unknown authorship, supposedly with a historical basis, but serving usually to explain some phenomenon of nature, the origin of Man, or the customs, religious rites, etc., of a people. Myths usually involve the feats of gods and heroes. Page 14.

N

name of the tree: the *bodhi tree,* a fig tree of India, which grows to a great age. Gautama Siddhartha (ca. 563–483? B.C.), the founder of Buddhism, achieved enlightenment while sitting under a bodhi tree and thus it has special significance and is held sacred by Buddhists. Page 133.

Napoleon: Napoleon Bonaparte (1769–1821), French military leader. He rose to power in France by military force, declared himself emperor and conducted campaigns of conquest across Europe. A defeat in 1814 led to his exile to a small island off the northwestern coast of Italy. After a brief return to power and final defeat in 1815, he was imprisoned on the tiny, mountainous island of St. Helena, in the South Atlantic Ocean. Page 106.

Natural Philosophy: the study of nature and the physical universe or of natural objects and phenomena. Page 125.

natural selection: the process by which forms of life having traits that better enable them to adapt to specific environmental pressures, such as predators, changes in climate, competition for food or mates, will tend to survive and reproduce in greater numbers than others of their kind, thus ensuring the perpetuation of those favorable traits in succeeding generations. Page 22.

Nature: the creative and regulative physical power which is conceived of as operating in the material world and as the immediate cause of all of its phenomena. Often represented as having human qualities or character, i.e., Mother Nature. Page 41.

nebulous: lacking definite form or limits; not clearly defined or described; vague. Page 120.

nerve: boldness; strength and endurance in a difficult or painful situation. Page 145.

neural: of or pertaining to a nerve or the nervous system. Page 31.

neurological: of or relating to matters affecting the nerves and the nervous system. Page 77.

neurologist: a physician trained in the field of *neurology,* the branch of medicine dealing with the nervous system and its diseases. Page 77.

Newton: Isaac Newton (1642–1727), English scientist and mathematician whose discoveries and theories laid the foundation for much of the scientific progress since his time. Newton made major contributions to the understanding of light, motion and gravity. Page 20.

nexus: the core, center or focus of something. Page 52.

niche: a small space set back in a wall; a secret place. Page 13.

Nietzsche: Friedrich Nietzsche (1844–1900), German philosopher and poet. He denounced all religion and promoted the "morals of masters," the doctrine of perfecting Man through forcible self-assertion and glorification of the "superman." Nietzsche declared that traditional values represented a slave morality and proclaimed that "God is dead." Page 88.

nineteenth-century psychology: modern psychology, formulated in the nineteenth century from the work of Wilhelm Wundt (1832–1920), German psychologist and physiologist (specialist in the study of the functions of physical, living things and the ways in which their parts and organs work). His work pushed a physiological basis for psychology and the false doctrine that Man is no more than an animal. Page 62.

Nirvana: in Buddhism and Hinduism, the state of freedom from worldly desires, the extinction of the individual existence and absorption into the Supreme Spirit, bringing an end to the endless cycle of birth and rebirth and its attendant suffering. Page 131.

nominally: being such in name only, not in fact. Page 100.

Northwest: the northwestern part of the United States, including Washington, Oregon and Idaho. Used here specifically in reference to Washington. Page 84.

Northwest Coast Indian lands: lands settled by Northwest Coast peoples, including the Tlingit, Chinook and Haida, encompassing more than 2,000 miles (3,200 kilometers) of the Pacific coast, from present-day southern Alaska to northern California, including Vancouver Island and the Queen Charlotte Islands off the coast of British Columbia, Canada. Page 31.

nothing short of: nothing less than. Used to emphasize forcefully that something truly or definitely is as described. Page 100.

nuclear physics: that branch of physics that deals with the behavior, structure and component parts of the center of an atom (called a *nucleus*), which makes up almost all of the mass of the atom. Page 56.

O

O: used to show the earnestness of an appeal, as expressive of longing. Page 84.

Oak Knoll Naval Hospital: a naval hospital located in Oakland, California, where LRH spent time recovering from injuries sustained during World War II (1939–1945) and researching the effect of the mind on the physical recovery of patients. Page 31.

oblivion: destruction or extinction. Also, a state of complete forgetfulness or unawareness. Page 115.

observatory: a building equipped with a large telescope for the scientific study of planets and stars. Page 20.

Occidental: of or characteristic of the *West,* the countries of Europe and the Americas. Page 83.

odyssey: a long and eventful or adventurous journey or process; an extensive intellectual or spiritual wandering or quest. From the ancient Greek poem of the same name, in which the poet Homer describes the adventures of Odysseus. *See also* **Homer.** Page 75.

old, of: from an earlier time or period. Page 115.

old-time: characteristic of someone whose experience goes back to past times or who is of long standing in a place or position. Page 122.

Old West: the American West during the 1800s, one of the last areas of the United States to be settled. Land was sparsely populated; livings were made through hard work, usually on farms, using basic tools; and the gun and the knife were used to capture available food and as a means of protection. The area and time is popularly thought of as a lawless frontier. Page 139.

-ologies: *-ology* means study or knowledge, usually in reference to any science or branch of knowledge; for example, biology (study of living organisms), geology (study of the physical history of Earth) or ethnology (study of the races of humankind). Page 79.

onslaught: a very large quantity of people or things that is difficult to deal with, likened to a powerful attack that overwhelms someone or something. Page 79.

open mind: having or showing a mind receptive to new ideas or arguments; impartial. Page 99.

Operating Thetan: by "Operating" is meant "able to act and handle things" and by "Thetan" is meant the spiritual being that is the basic self. "Theta" is Greek for thought or Life or the spirit. An Operating Thetan, then, is one who can handle things without having to use a body of physical means. Page 122.

Operating Thetan, Symbol of: the Symbol of Operating Thetan is an oval crossed by a horizontal bar, with a vertical bar down from its center to the bottom of the oval. By "Operating" is meant "able to act and handle things" and by "Thetan" is meant the spiritual being that is the basic self. "Theta" is Greek for thought or Life or the spirit. An Operating Thetan, then, is one who can handle things without having to use a body of physical means. Page 3.

optic nerve(s): the nerve that carries signals from the eye to the brain. *Optic* means of or relating to the eye or vision. Page 149.

oratorical: of, relating to or characteristic of an *orator,* one who delivers a formal speech. Page 88.

order of, on the: resembling to some extent; like. Page 33.

Organizational Chart: also called *Organizing Board,* a large chart used in Churches of Scientology. The chart or board is laid out in an exact pattern. It displays the functions, duties, sequences of action and authorities of the organization. Page 108.

Orient: the countries of eastern Asia, especially China, Japan and their neighbors. Page 83.

orthodox: conforming to the usual beliefs or established doctrines. Page 52.

orthodoxy: the state of being *orthodox.* Page 101.

oscilloscope: an electronic instrument that displays changing electrical signals. The signals appear as wavy lines or in other patterns on a screen. Page 53.

OT Course: a program leading to the state of Operating Thetan. By "Operating" is meant "able to act and handle things" and by "Thetan" is meant the spiritual being that is the basic self. "Theta" is Greek for thought or Life or the spirit. An Operating Thetan, then, is one who can handle things without having to use a body of physical means. Page 134.

outpost(s): an outlying or remote branch. Page 108.

outworn: no longer useful or accepted; outmoded; obsolete. Page 22.

overarching: embracive and all-encompassing, likened to a curved structure (arch) that spans or extends across the entire width or space of something. Page 75.

overweather, stratosphere and: a reference to aircraft capable of flying in the *stratosphere,* an atmospheric zone reaching from about 12 to 30 miles (20 to 50 kilometers) above the Earth's surface. This altitude is high enough that the aircraft is above the clouds, or "over the weather." Aircraft that could fly high enough to get above the weather began being built in the 1940s. Page 25.

P

painstaking: done with great care and thoroughness. Page 13.

pantheon: a group of people who are the most famous or respected in a particular field. Page 124.

paramount: more important than anything else; supreme. Page 24.

Parmenides: (515?–450? B.C.) Greek philosopher, considered by many to be the most important of the early Greek philosophers before Socrates. Parmenides deduced the nature of reality from logical argument, unlike previous Greek philosophers, who explained the origin of the world in terms of material substances, such as air or water. Page 125.

passes for: is accepted as or believed to be. Often used with the implication of actually being something else. Page 2.

Pasteur: Louis Pasteur (1822–1895), French chemist who in the late 1800s formulated *the germ theory of disease,* that disease was spread by germs attacking the body. He was noted for his discovery that the desired production of alcohol in the process of fermentation is indeed due to yeast (a small single-celled organism). He found that wine turns bitter because of germs that enter the wine while it is being made and showed these germs can be killed by applying controlled heat. This became known as *pasteurization* and was also applied to killing the germs in milk. (*Fermentation* is a chemical process that breaks down organic materials, such as when the microscopic organism yeast breaks down sugar into alcohol and carbon dioxide gas.) Page 41.

pawn: something that can be used for one's advantage. Page 63.

pay one's way: pay one's own expenses. Page 89.

Pelley: William Dudley Pelley (1890–1965), American author. In 1928, Pelley claimed to have had an out-of-body experience, which he detailed in the pamphlet "My Seven Minutes in Eternity." Page 85.

perchance: perhaps; possibly. Page 84.

perilous: very dangerous; involving exposure to very great danger. Page 115.

personage: a person; a person of distinction. Page 106.

perspective: a specific point of view in understanding or judging things or events, especially one that shows them in their true relations to one another. Page 10.

philosopher: one who studies or practices philosophy. *See also* **philosophy.** Page 2.

philosophy: the love, study or pursuit of wisdom, or of knowledge of things and their causes, whether theoretical or practical; the study of the truths or principles underlying all knowledge, being (reality) or conduct. From Greek *philos,* loving, and *sophia,* learning. Page 1.

Phoenicians: the inhabitants of *Phoenicia,* an ancient kingdom at the eastern end of the Mediterranean Sea, famous for its far-reaching trade. Located in present-day Syria and Lebanon. Page 26.

Phoenix, Arizona: a city in and capital of Arizona, a state in the southwestern United States. During the early and mid-1950s, LRH gave approximately five hundred recorded lectures in Phoenix. Page 51.

phonograph record: a vinyl disc (normally 12 inches in diameter) with grooves (indentations) in it, on which music, voice or other sounds are recorded. A needle is lowered upon the disc which is spinning on a rotating, round table. The needle fits in the grooves of the record and transfers the sound recorded in the grooves to speakers for playback. Page 42.

photometer: an instrument for measuring the intensity of light. Page 81.

physics: the science that deals with matter, energy, motion and force, including what these things are, why they behave as they do and the relationship between them. Page 22.

picture of the picture…on the cereal box: a reference to the packaging for the oat cereal produced by the Quaker Oats Company, an international manufacturer of grocery products. The Quaker

Oats box displayed a Quaker (a member of a Christian denomination founded in England in the seventeenth century) dressed in eighteenth-century clothing with a broad-brimmed black hat, holding a Quaker Oats box, upon which was the same (but smaller) picture of the Quaker holding a Quaker Oats box and so on. Page 83.

pinnacle: the highest or topmost point or level of something. Page 53.

pitfall(s): a hidden or unexpected disaster or difficulty. From the literal idea of a *pitfall,* a trap that is a deep hole in the ground (pit) disguised with leaves covering its top opening and having sides so steep that escape is impossible. Page 117.

pivotal: of vital or critical importance. Page 9.

plane: a level of existence, consciousness or development. Page 37.

platitudes: dull, unoriginal or empty statements on a moral theme, especially those expressed as if they were important or helpful. Page 2.

Plato: (427?–347 B.C.) Greek philosopher noted for his works on law, mathematics, technical philosophic problems and natural science. One of his most important works, the *Republic,* written in the form of a dialogue, is an inquiry into the nature of justice and the organization of a perfect society. Page 22.

plight: a bad, unfortunate or even dangerous condition, state or situation. Page 124.

plunged: brought or forced suddenly into an unpleasant or undesirable situation. Page 132.

point of fact, in: with regard to matters of fact. Page 52.

point of jump-off: a place to start from, as of a journey, course of action, line of reasoning, etc. Page 88.

polio: short for *poliomyelitis,* a highly infectious disease, widespread in the 1950s, that usually occurred in children and young adults. It affected the brain and spinal cord, sometimes leading to a loss of voluntary movement and muscular wasting (loss of muscular strength or substance). Page 102.

polish up: make improvements in. Page 21.

political: of or having to do with *politics,* the science or practice of government; the regulation and government of a nation or state for the preservation of its safety, peace and prosperity. *Government* is that controlling body of a nation, state or people which conducts its policy, actions and affairs. Page 22.

political ends: goals or results (ends) of a political nature. *Political* in this context means characterized by dishonest practices used to ensure that a certain form of government or group of people maintains or wins control. Page 7.

Polo, Marco: (1254–1324) traveler and author from Venice, Italy, whose account of his travels and experiences in China offered Europeans a firsthand view of Asian lands and stimulated interest in Asian trade. Page 75.

poltergeist: manifestations or activities similar to those of *poltergeists,* ghosts that manifest themselves by noises, rappings, invisibly moving things, etc. *Poltergeist* comes from German *poltern,* to make noises, and *geist,* ghost. Page 123.

polysyllabic: consisting of several, especially four or more, syllables (words or parts of words pronounced with a single, uninterrupted sounding of the voice), such large words sometimes being employed by those who act very learned and serious. Page 83.

Porch of Maidens: a part of a temple on the Acropolis, built between 421 and 406 B.C. to honor legendary founders of Athens and to house the city's most sacred object, an ancient statue of Athena, the patron goddess and protector of Athens. The supporting columns of the porch are sculptures of maidens, believed to represent young women who would take part in a religious procession honoring the goddess. Page 133.

Port Orchard: a resort and fishing community located in western Washington State on *Puget Sound,* a long, narrow bay of the Pacific Ocean on the northwestern coast of the United States. Page 7.

Portsmouth: a reference to Portsmouth Naval Prison, part of the Portsmouth Naval Shipyard, a naval shipyard built in the 1790s and located in Kittery, Maine. Kittery is situated across the Piscataqua River from Portsmouth, New Hampshire. Both Portsmouth and Kittery were founded in 1623 and have been important ports for fishing and shipbuilding. Page 89.

positron(s): an elementary particle having some of the same properties as an electron but having a positive charge (as opposed to the negative charge of an electron). It is not part of an atom. When a positron contacts an electron, it creates energy. Also called an *antielectron.* Page 23.

Power Elite: a closely knit alliance of military, government and corporate officials perceived as the center of wealth and political power in the US. Page 136.

precipitously: in a sudden and dramatic manner; hastily. Page 92.

preclear: from *pre-Clear,* a person not yet Clear; generally a person being audited, who is thus on the road to *Clear,* the name of a state achieved through auditing or an individual who has achieved this state. The Clear is an unaberrated person. He is rational in that he forms the best possible solutions he can on the data he has and from his viewpoint. Page 106.

prefatory: of, pertaining to or of the nature of a *preface,* a preliminary statement in a book by an author or editor, setting forth its purpose and scope, etc. Page 10.

prejudices: judgments or opinions held in disregard of facts that contradict them; unreasonable biases. Page 139.

preponderance: weight, force, importance or influence. Page 132.

prerevolutionary China: a reference to China in the period from roughly 1928 until 1949. During this time the government was controlled by the Chinese *Nationalists,* the political party that had overturned the emperor (1911) and established China as a nation with elected leaders. After 1928, the Nationalists tried to block a revolution by the increasingly powerful Chinese Communists. A civil war eventually broke out. By 1949, with a Communist victory assured, the Nationalists moved to Taiwan, an island off the southeast coast of China, and set up a separate government. Page 75.

presumable: assumed to be correct or workable without close inspection. Page 41.

presumptuous: showing overconfidence or arrogance. Page 55.

Prime Mover Unmoved: according to the philosophy of Aristotle (384–322 B.C.), that which is the first cause of all motion in the universe, which itself does not move; that eternal, immaterial and unchangeable thing which Aristotle considered to be divine thought, mind or God. Page 23.

probing: searching into or examining thoroughly, as if by penetrating deeply into unknown or obscure points or parts. Page 68.

processing: the application of Dianetics or Scientology techniques (called *processes*). Processes are directly concerned with increasing the ability of the individual to survive, with increasing his sanity or ability to reason, his physical ability and his general enjoyment of life. Also called *auditing.* Page 53.

progenitor(s): someone who develops something; an originator. Page 124.

prone to: likely to or liable to suffer from, do or experience something, typically something regrettable or unwelcome. Page 106.

pronouncement: a formal opinion, declaration, decision or statement of fact. Page 155.

propagandize: disseminate or spread by *propaganda,* information, beliefs or ideas deliberately spread widely to help or harm a person, group, movement, nation, etc. Page 22.

proposition: a statement about something being considered or discussed. Page 102.

prose: ordinary written language, in contrast to poetry. Page 81.

protagonist: the most important character in a novel, play, story or other literary work. Page 18.

prototypic: of or being a *prototype,* the original or model on which other things are based or formed. Page 68.

provocatively: in a manner that calls forth or stimulates discussion, anticipation, interest or the like. Page 2.

pseudo: not actually, but having the appearance of; pretended; false. Page 26.

psychoses: conflicts of commands which seriously reduce the individual's ability to solve his problems in his environment to a point where he cannot adjust himself to some vital phase of his environmental needs. Page 42.

psychosomatic: *psycho* refers to mind and *somatic* refers to body; the term *psychosomatic* means the mind making the body ill or illnesses which have been created physically within the body by the mind. A description of the cause and source of psychosomatic ills is contained in *Dianetics: The Modern Science of Mental Health*. Page 35.

psychosurgery: use of brain surgery as a supposed treatment of mental disorders. Page 76.

Ptolemy: Claudius Ptolomaeus, second-century A.D. mathematician, astronomer and geographer in Alexandria, Egypt. His geometric theories explained the apparent motions and positions of the planets, Sun and Moon. He stated that while these bodies move, the stars do not. Page 20.

public property: something that is available to a person, a group of persons, the community or the public. Used figuratively. Page 138.

Puget Sound: a long, narrow bay of the Pacific Ocean on the coast of Washington, a state in the northwestern United States. Page 7.

punched protein molecules: perforated molecules in the body or mind that were believed to store memories. Page 84.

pygmy: any of a people of very small size. Page 143.

Pythagoras: (582–500 B.C.) Greek philosopher and mathematician who founded a school in southern Italy that emphasized the study of musical harmony and geometry and is considered the first true mathematician. Page 20.

Q

quest(s): a search or pursuit, especially a long or difficult one, made in order to find or obtain something that is greatly desired. Page 1.

quiet: calm somebody's feelings, such as doubts or fears. Page 14.

R

realize: make real; give reality to. Page 2.

realm: the region or sphere within which anything occurs or dominates. Page 7.

ream(s): a large quantity of written material. From the literal meaning of *ream,* a quantity of paper, now usually 500 sheets (formerly 480 sheets). Page 116.

rear guard: the rear (back) portion of an advancing army or armed force. Hence any group of people who, rather than lead, trail far behind others in new developments, ideas or actions. Page 56.

rebirth: a new or second birth. Page 101.

rebuff: an abrupt, blunt refusal, as of offered advice or help. Page 79.

recalled (to): brought back to matters previously considered. Page 84.

recorder: *tape recorder,* a machine for recording sound as electrical signals on *magnetic tape,* a thin ribbon of material, usually plastic, coated with metal particles that become magnetized and thus record sounds. Page 92.

record, phonograph: a vinyl disc (normally 12 inches in diameter) with grooves (indentations) in it, on which music, voice or other sounds are recorded. A needle is lowered upon the disc which is spinning on a rotating, round table. The needle fits in the grooves of the record and transfers the sound recorded in the grooves to speakers for playback. Page 42.

redeemed: made up for or offset the faults or bad aspects of something. Page 56.

red flag: something serving as a warning of trouble or danger ahead. Page 22.

regale(d): entertain or amuse someone in a highly agreeable manner. Page 84.

regressive: moving back into a worse condition; declining. Page 42.

reiterate: say again; repeat. Page 53.

relapse: return to a former state, especially an undesirable one, after coming out of it for a while. Page 35.

Remington: a typewriter manufactured by the Remington & Sons company of New York. Remington typewriters were first produced in the early 1870s. A manual typewriter requires no electricity to operate. Page 44.

rendered: caused to be or become; made. Page 37.

renegade: of or like a *renegade,* a person who goes against or betrays the principles of an organization or country; disloyal. Page 136.

replete: well supplied (with something). Page 44.

repository: a storehouse; a source or supply of something. Page 76.

reproduction: the action or process of copying an original; duplication. Page 92.

Republic: one of the most important works of Plato (427?–347 B.C.), Greek philosopher noted for his works on law, mathematics, technical philosophic problems and natural science. The *Republic,* written in the form of a dialogue, is an inquiry into the nature of justice and the organization of a perfect society. Page 22.

repute: favorable reputation; good name; public respect. Page 142.

resigned: gave up an office or position, often formally. Page 137.

resurrection: the act of rising from the dead or coming back to life. Page 101.

retreat: a quiet place where a person can go for privacy. Page 7.

retrospective: marked by a looking back over past situations, events, etc. Page 75.

revelation: an action or instance of the showing or revealing of the truth about something. Page 3.

revere: feel deep respect or admiration for (someone or something). Page 120.

reverence: deep respect shown toward someone or something. Page 20.

revivalist: dedicated to reawakening or stimulating religious fervor, such as through *faith healing,* healing brought about through prayer or religious faith. Page 52.

riddle: something that is difficult to understand or presents a problem that needs to be solved. Page 33.

riveted: fixed or held the attention firmly, as if by means of a *rivet,* a fastener in the form of a short metal rod with a head. The shaft is passed through holes in materials and flattened into a second head on the other side. Page 102.

Rogers, Donald: a staff member who worked at the Dianetic Foundation in Elizabeth, New Jersey, in the early 1950s. Page 100.

roll of genetic dice, dumb: ignorant (dumb) throw of the dice, as in a gambling game. A *"dumb roll of the genetic dice"* likens *genetics,* the science that deals with the passing on of genetic factors (such as the color of hair or eyes) from one generation to the next, resulting in similarities between members of one family, to the uncertainty of a gambling game. Page 10.

roped: caught an animal by throwing a circle of rope around it. Page 140.

rough and tumble: characterized by rough informality or disregard of usual rules; roughly vigorous. Page 139.

royalties: payments to an author, composer or inventor consisting of a percentage of the income from the individual's book, piece of music or invention. Page 137.

rubber-stamped: tending to give routine approval or authorization (of proposals, actions, etc.) automatically or without appropriate consideration. Page 24.

rung of the ladder, first: the very bottom (lowest) level. A *rung* is any of the steps of a ladder and is used figuratively to suggest a state, level or position. Page 134.

run out: exhausted the negative influence of something; erased. Page 106.

S

sage(s): a man of deep wisdom. Page 65.

Saint Hill: a manor (a large house and its land) located in East Grinstead, Sussex, in southern England. Saint Hill Manor was the residence of L. Ron Hubbard as well as the international communications and training center of Scientology from the late 1950s through the mid-1960s. Page 115.

saint(s): somebody who has been particularly holy in life and after death is declared by a Christian church to have a privileged place in Heaven and be worthy of worship. Also, someone who is a particularly good or holy person, or one who is extremely kind and patient in dealing with difficult people or situations. Page 120.

salient: that stands out as important; particularly relevant. Page 75.

salt mines: mines from which salt is excavated, with allusion to the practice of sentencing offenders to labor in a salt mine; so referring to any place of habitual confinement or drudgery. Page 82.

Sanscrit: also *Sanskrit,* the ancient and sacred language of India, with its own distinctive alphabet, maintained as the literary language of the priestly, learned and cultivated groups in Indian society. Page 20.

savages: uncivilized human beings. Page 145.

savants: persons of extensive learning; learned scholars. Page 120.

Savior: a name used by Christians for the teacher and prophet Jesus Christ. Page 52.

scant: barely sufficient or adequate. Page 20.

scheme of things: the way everything in the world seems to be organized; an apparent overall system within which everything has a place. Page 141.

schooner: a sailing ship with sails set lengthwise (fore and aft) and having from two to as many as seven masts. Page 139.

Schopenhauer: Arthur Schopenhauer (1788–1860), German philosopher who believed that the will to live is the fundamental reality and that this will, being a constant striving, cannot be satisfied and only causes suffering. Page 20.

science: knowledge; comprehension or understanding of facts or principles, classified and made available in work, life or the search for truth. A science is a connected body of demonstrated truths or observed facts systematically organized and bound together under general laws. It includes trustworthy methods for the discovery of new truth within its domain and denotes the application of scientific methods in fields of study previously considered open only to theories based on subjective, historical or undemonstrable, abstract criteria. The word *science* is used in this sense—the most fundamental meaning and tradition of the word—and not in the sense of the *physical* or *material* sciences. Page 10.

science of (mind): in such uses as *science of art, science of mind,* the application of scientific methods in fields of study formerly considered open only to theories based on opinion or abstract data which cannot be proven or demonstrated. Page 35.

Scientology: Scientology is the study and handling of the spirit in relationship to itself, universes and other life. The term Scientology is taken from the Latin *scio,* which means "knowing in the fullest sense of the word," and the Greek word *logos,* meaning "study of." In itself the word means literally "knowing how to know." Page 1.

Scientology 8-80: a book written by L. Ron Hubbard, first published in 1952, that gives the first explanation of the electronics of human thought and the energy phenomena in any being. Page 68.

Scientology Cross: the Scientology Cross is an eight-pointed cross representing the eight dynamics of life through which each individual is striving to survive: (1) self; (2) sex, the family and the future generation; (3) groups; (4) Mankind; (5) life, all organisms; (6) matter, energy, space and time—MEST—the physical universe; (7) spirits; and (8) the Supreme Being. In *Dianetics: The Modern Science of Mental Health* the first four dynamics are described, because Dianetics covers the first four dynamics. Scientology covers all eight dynamics. Page 3.

Scientology Symbol: the Scientology Symbol consists of the letter *S*, for Scientology, which is derived from *scio*, knowing in the fullest sense of the word. The lower triangle is the *ARC Triangle*, its points being affinity, reality and communication, which combined give understanding. The upper triangle is the *KRC Triangle*, its points being knowledge, responsibility and control. By increasing each point of these triangles, little by little, one can increase understanding and accomplishment. Page 2.

scraped the surface: variation of *scratched the surface*, made only slight progress in understanding, taking effective action on, etc.; not penetrated very far into. Page 19.

scrapheap: a place for dumping old, useless things. Page 147.

scribe: a writer or author, such as someone in ancient times who wrote histories or other works. Page 13.

seal(s): a stamp used to certify a signature or show that a document is legal. The seal has a design that is cut below the surface. Seals are pressed into wax or directly into paper, leaving the impression of the design on the wax or paper to indicate that the document is authentic. Page 68.

sea of ammonia: a reference to one of the evolutionary theories of the "origin of life" on this planet. Per this theory, life arose through a series of spontaneous chemical reactions involving various substances, including ammonia. The theory supposes these compounds fell from the atmosphere into the sea, interacted and grew larger and larger. Somehow, cells were formed, which eventually led to the life forms that inhabit Earth today, including Man. Page 129.

Second Synod of Constantinople: an assembly of Christian Church delegates (synod) that met in 553 A.D. to settle points of Church doctrine. The Second Synod declared certain views heretical—for example, that the soul existed before birth and that a purified soul would go to Heaven, that there was no Hell and that there was no resurrection of the body. Such views were contrary to the doctrine of the Church, which held that the soul did not exist before birth, that there is Hell and that, after a general judgment of the human race, the body and soul, reunited, would be resurrected. Page 101.

self-centered: concerned solely or chiefly with one's own interests, welfare, etc.; selfish. Page 137.

seminal: being among the first or earliest of something. Page 51.

service record: the record of a person's employment in a branch of military service. For example, a naval service record contains documents such as birth certificate, school certificates, letters of commendation, enlistment contract, history of assignments, performance record, medical record, rank, etc. Page 149.

severely: strictly; precisely and only. Page 80.

shades: the departed spirits of the dead collectively; also the world of the dead. Page 11.

shake: figuratively, strike with jarring, unsettling impact as in causing change in something, such as society or civilization, that usually resists change or changes only very slowly. Page 100.

shaken: disturbed or upset. Page 11.

sham: something that is presented as genuine but that is not. Page 52.

shed light on: help to explain by providing further information; make clear. Page 137.

shelf, on the: put aside or not being actively worked on. Page 18.

shots: small amounts of a strong alcoholic drink. Page 84.

shrugging off (something): dismissing something as unimportant. Page 129.

sidelight: a piece of incidental information on a subject, usually adding to what is already known. Literally, light coming from the side. Page 106.

sight unseen: without seeing or inspecting first. Page 52.

singularly: extraordinarily; remarkably; to an unusual degree or extent. Page 142.

slain: killed. Page 129.

slanderous: characterized by *slander*, false spoken statements about someone that are intended to damage the good opinion that people have of him. Page 142.

slave master: one who dominates or controls others, likened to someone who owns other persons who have no freedom or personal rights. Page 148.

slipping through the Curtain: *slipping* means moving or passing quietly, easily and quickly. A *curtain* is a piece of cloth or similar material that serves to cover or conceal what is behind it. Used here figuratively to refer to the unconsciousness of death. Page 11.

slither: slide or creep as would a snake. Page 130.

soaring plane: a motorless plane that uses upward air currents to stay aloft, often soaring for several hours at a time. Such aircraft are usually towed to the correct altitude by another aircraft, as an airplane, or by an automobile. Page 82.

Socrates: (470?–399 B.C.) Greek philosopher and teacher and one of the most original and influential figures in ancient Greek philosophy and in the history of Western thought. Before Socrates, Greek philosophy focused on the nature and origin of the universe. He redirected philosophy toward a consideration of moral problems and how people should best live their lives. Page 125.

soft ways: gentle, mild, warm-hearted or compassionate conduct or habitual manner. Page 139.

sound: 1. free from disease or injury; healthy. Page 36.
2. seem to be; give the appearance of being. Page 81.
3. based on good sense and valid reasoning. Page 90.

South Pacific: the region of the Pacific Ocean lying south of the equator, including its islands. It extends southward from the equator to Antarctica. Page 139.

spanning: the action or an instance of something extending or reaching across from one point to another. Page 150.

sparking: emitting or producing *sparks,* bright streaks or flashes of light, as from equipment. Page 24.

speak-easy: a place where alcoholic beverages were sold and consumed during *Prohibition,* a period in the United States (1920–1933) in which the manufacture, transportation and sale of alcoholic liquors for beverage purposes were forbidden by federal law. Many people ignored the national ban. Page 84.

special-interest group: a group of people or an organization seeking or receiving special advantages or treatment, typically through persuading political representatives or influential persons to issue laws in their favor. Page 143.

specialization: the process of becoming an expert in a particular skill, area of study or function; concentration on a particular activity or product. Page 24.

speculative: of writing that is usually considered to include fantasy, horror, science fiction and the like, dealing with worlds unlike the real world. Page 18.

Spencer, Herbert: (1820–1903) English philosopher known for his application of the scientific doctrines of evolution to philosophy and ethics. Spencer claimed that knowledge was of two kinds: (1) knowledge gained by the individual, and (2) knowledge gained by the race. He also believed that there is a basic and final reality beyond our knowledge, which he called the "Unknowable." Page 7.

spent: used up or consumed. Page 116.

Spinoza: Benedict Spinoza (1632–1677), Dutch philosopher and religious thinker. He believed that Man's highest happiness consists in coming to understand and appreciate the truth that he is a tiny part of a god who is present in everything. Page 18.

splendor: magnificent richness or glory. Page 75.

splitting the atom: the splitting of atomic nuclei (the central region of atoms, consisting of minute, tightly-bound particles and containing most of the mass) and the subsequent release of vast amounts of energy as observed in a nuclear reaction. In the early 1930s, scientists in Cambridge, England, became the first to split the atom. Page 23.

spontaneous combustion: a humorous reference to *spontaneous generation,* the view that certain forms of life can develop directly from nonliving things. The Greeks believed that flies and other small animals arose from the mud at the bottom of streams and ponds; this has been carried forward by most scientists in the theory that spontaneous generation took place when certain chemicals somehow came together in mud to form the first simple living organism billions of years ago. A cell was eventually formed that collided with other cells and through accident formed a more complex organism—eventually leading to the appearance of Man. (*Spontaneous* means having no apparent external cause or influence; occurring or produced by its own energy, force, etc.; self-acting.) Page 129.

sported: displayed, presented, had available or the like. Page 85.

spurned: rejected with contempt. Page 21.

St. Elizabeths Hospital: a government-funded psychiatric hospital (state institution) for the mentally ill and criminally insane, founded in the mid-1800s in Washington, DC. Page 76.

stable(s): a group or staff of writers engaged to contribute their services when called upon; pool. Page 33.

star shell: an artillery shell timed to burst in midair in a shower of bright particles that light up the surrounding terrain. Page 21.

stem: stop, check or restrain. Page 79.

stemming from: originating or developing as the result of something. Page 102.

stepchild: something junior to and indirectly related to something else in a similar manner as the child of one's spouse from a previous marriage. Page 18.

steppingstone: a stage or step that helps achieve a goal. Page 10.

stimulus-response: a certain stimulus (something that rouses a person or thing to activity or energy or that produces a reaction in the body) automatically giving a certain response. Page 37.

sting, lose its: remove the pain from a sting. Figuratively, *sting* means anything with the capacity or power to inflict mental pain or distress. Thus *"the threat of eternal damnation tended to lose its sting"* means it lost its power to produce pain or upset. Page 101.

Story of Philosophy, The: the title of a book, published in 1926, by American author, historian and popularizer of philosophy Will Durant (1885–1981). The book explains in simple language the central ideas of the world's greatest philosophers and tells of their lives. Despite criticism from many critics and scholars who condemned the book for its simplified style, easily comprehensible to the average reader, *The Story of Philosophy* was immensely popular, selling millions of copies in a dozen languages. Page 147.

strain(s): a distinct breed, stock or variety of an animal, plant or other organism. Page 9.

stratosphere and overweather: a reference to aircraft capable of flying in the *stratosphere,* an atmospheric zone reaching from about 12 to 30 miles (20 to 50 kilometers) above the Earth's surface. This altitude is high enough that the aircraft is above the clouds, or "over the weather." Aircraft that could fly high enough to get above the weather began being built in the 1940s. Page 25.

street piano: a mechanical piano fitted with wheels, operated by turning a crank and played on the streets. Such instruments are said to have first been made in England, in the early nineteenth century. Page 106.

strewn: has (something) scattered through it. Page 144.

stumbling block: an obstacle or hindrance to progress or understanding. Page 129.

subjective: existing in the mind; dependent on the mind or on an individual's perception for its existence, as opposed to objective. Page 132.

subject to: open to or liable to suffer from something unsettling, unfavorable or damaging. Page 20.

succinct: briefly and clearly expressed. Page 132.

suffice: meet present needs or requirements; be sufficient. Page 145.

superimposed: imposed or placed on or upon another; laid above or on the top. *Super-* means over, above or on and *impose* means to place on or onto. Page 77.

superintendent: a person who oversees or directs some work, enterprise, establishment, organization, district, etc.; supervisor. Page 76.

surface, scraped the: variation of *scratched the surface,* made only slight progress in understanding, taking effective action on, etc.; not penetrated very far into. Page 19.

surveying: the science or work of determining the location, form or boundaries of an area of land by measuring the lines and angles, often to make up engineering designs showing how various structures will be built. Page 83.

Sussex: a former county of southeastern England, now divided into two counties, East Sussex and West Sussex. Saint Hill is located in East Grinstead, West Sussex. Page 115.

swamped: overwhelmed, especially overwhelmed with an excess of something. Page 23.

swamping sea (of facts): overwhelming by being too many (facts) to cope with, likened to a body of water that overwhelms a ship. Page 24.

symbiote(s): any entity of life or energy which assists an individual or Man in his survival. Page 36.

Symbol, Dianetics: the Dianetics Symbol uses the triangular shape of the Greek letter *delta* as its basic form. It is made up of stripes of green (which stands for growth) and stripes of yellow (which stands for life). The four green stripes represent the four dynamics of Dianetics: survival as (I) self, (II) sex and family, (III) group and (IV) Mankind. Page 2.

Symbol of Operating Thetan: the Symbol of Operating Thetan is an oval crossed by a horizontal bar, with a vertical bar down from its center to the bottom of the oval. By "Operating" is meant "able to act and handle things" and by "Thetan" is meant the spiritual being that is the basic self. "Theta" is Greek for thought or Life or the spirit. An Operating Thetan, then, is one who can handle things without having to use a body of physical means. Page 3.

symbol of Scientology Cross: the Scientology Cross is an eight-pointed cross representing the eight dynamics of life through which each individual is striving to survive: (1) self; (2) sex, the family and the future generation; (3) groups; (4) Mankind; (5) life, all organisms; (6) matter, energy, space and time—MEST—the physical universe; (7) spirits; and (8) the Supreme Being. In *Dianetics: The Modern Science of Mental Health* the first four dynamics are described, because Dianetics covers the first four dynamics. Scientology covers all eight dynamics. Page 3.

Symbol, Scientology: the Scientology Symbol consists of the letter *S,* for Scientology, which is derived from *scio,* knowing in the fullest sense of the word. The lower triangle is the *ARC Triangle,* its points being affinity, reality and communication, which combined give understanding. The upper triangle is the *KRC Triangle,* its points being knowledge, responsibility and control. By increasing each point of these triangles, little by little, one can increase understanding and accomplishment. Page 2.

symmetry: correspondence of opposite parts in size, shape, position or the like; regularity of form or arrangement in terms of like or corresponding parts. Page 81.

synaptic: of or having to do with the *synapses,* the minute spaces between nerve cells, muscle cells, etc., through which nerve impulses are transmitted from one to the other. Page 77.

synopsis: a brief or condensed statement giving a general view of something. Page 33.

Synthetic Philosophy: a reference to *A System of Synthetic Philosophy,* a work by English philosopher Herbert Spencer (1820–1903), in which he outlined a plan for a comprehensive system of philosophy, based on evolution, that would embrace and integrate all existing fields of knowledge. Page 7.

T

tamper: make changes in something for some purpose. Page 80.

tangentially: in a way that has only slight relevance to some other topic or subject. Page 18.

Tao: the word *Tao* means the way to knowledge. Page 65.

Taoists: those who follow the doctrines of *Taoism,* a Chinese philosophical and religious system, dating from about the fourth century B.C., based on the doctrine of Lao-tzu (ca. sixth century B.C.), one of the great philosophers of China. *Tao* means the way to knowledge. Page 65.

"taunting": driving or forcing something, as a response, by or as if by irritating or bothering something. Page 9.

Technical Bulletin(s): a type of issue written by L. Ron Hubbard. These issues are technical (relating to Scientology technology) and contain all data for auditing and courses. They are printed in red ink on white paper, consecutive by date, and are distributed as indicated, usually to technical staff. *See also* **technology.** Page 117.

technology: the methods of application of an art or science as opposed to mere knowledge of the science or art itself. In Scientology, the term *technology* refers to the methods of application of Scientology principles to improve the functions of the mind and rehabilitate the potentials of the spirit, developed by L. Ron Hubbard. Page 18.

tedium: boredom; condition or quality of being tiresome or monotonous. Page 81.

teleport: send or be sent by *teleportation,* the act of transporting or being transported across space and distance instantly. Page 18.

telex: a two-way communication system using a device similar to a typewriter which is used to type a message which is then transmitted electronically over telephone lines to another location where the message is printed out. *Telex* stands for "teleprinter exchange service." A *teleprinter* (also called a teletypewriter) is a typewriter-like device for transmitting messages as they are typed and for printing messages received. Page 111.

telling: revealing; that tells or reveals much. Page 33.

Terra Incognita: an unknown or unexplored land, region or subject. The term is Latin for "unknown land." Page 47.

terse: concise, brief. Page 33.

testosterone: the hormone that brings about masculine characteristics in the body. Synthetic versions of it were developed in the 1930s. Because these worked by accelerating the processes that build muscle tissue, they were used during World War II (1939–1945) to rebuild the body weight of concentration camp survivors and other war victims. Page 33.

Texas: a state in the southwest United States. Page 106.

Thales: (625?–546? B.C.) the earliest known Greek philosopher and the first philosopher to attempt to discover the underlying material source of all things, which he believed was water. Page 20.

theologian: a person knowledgeable in the field of *theology,* the study of religious matters and philosophy. Page 3.

therapy: the administration and application of Dianetics techniques and procedures to resolve problems concerning human behavior and psychosomatic illness. Page 31.

theta: the life force, life energy, divine energy, élan vital, or by any other name, the energy peculiar to life which acts upon material in the physical universe and animates it, mobilizes it and changes it. (From the Greek letter *theta,* θ, traditional philosopher's symbol of thought, spirit or life.) Page 55.

Theta Clear: a state wherein the spirit may knowingly and at will separate from the body. *See also* **exteriorization.** Page 55.

Thetan Exterior: a being who knows he is a spirit with a body and not just a body. Page 123.

Thompson, Commander Joseph Cheesman: (1874–1943) a commander and surgeon in the United States Navy who studied Freudian analysis with Sigmund Freud (1856–1939). Page 75.

Tibetan lamaseries: monasteries of *lamas,* priests or monks in *Lamaism,* a branch of Buddhism that seeks to find release from the suffering of life and attain a state of complete happiness and peace. Lamaism is practiced in Tibet, a land in south central Asia, and in areas such as Mongolia, a country to the north of China. Page 75.

tomes: books, especially very heavy, large or learned books. Page 23.

tongues: languages of particular peoples, regions or nations. Page 99.

"top down and the bottom up, the": *top* is the highest level or rank (within a society) and the *bottom* refers to the lowest level. *"The top down and the bottom up"* refers to LRH's study of existence at the highest and lowest levels of the society. Page 2.

tortuous: not direct; full of twists, turns or bends. Page 31.

towering: very important or influential. Page 144.

towers, artificial: variation of *ivory towers.* An *ivory tower* is a figurative reference to a separation from real-life problems; a state or situation in which somebody is sheltered from the practicalities or difficulties of ordinary life. Page 139.

to wit: used to introduce a list or explanation of what one has just mentioned. Originally a phrase used in law, *that is to wit,* which meant that is to know, that is to say. Page 33.

tract(s): a pamphlet produced for general distribution that sets out an opinion, position or an analysis, usually dealing with a moral, political or religious issue, in order to try to influence people's attitudes. Page 23.

tradition, in the: in keeping with a long-established way of thinking or acting. Page 65.

transcendent: going beyond ordinary limits or range—for example, of thought or belief; surpassing or exceeding the usual. Page 124.

transcends: goes beyond the limit or range of. Page 115.

transcribed: (of dictated material, notes or other spoken material) made a written copy, especially a typewritten copy, of. Page 108.

traversed: passed or moved over, along or through. Page 21.

tread, where the devil would fear to: a variation of the saying *Fools rush in where angels fear to tread,* meaning people with little experience or knowledge often get involved in difficult situations that those with superior wisdom and understanding avoid. This expression comes from a line in the poem *An Essay on Criticism* (1711) by English poet Alexander Pope (1688–1744), where he discusses the laws by which a critic should be guided and gives examples of critics who have violated these laws. By extension, a place *"where the devil would fear to tread"* is a place so dangerous that even a devil would not want to go there. Page 25.

treatise: a formal, usually extensive, written work on a subject. Page 20.

treatment: the practice of Dianetics techniques and procedures to resolve problems concerning human behavior and psychosomatic illness. Page 35.

tree, name of the: the *bodhi tree,* a fig tree of India, which grows to a great age. Gautama Siddhartha (563–483? B.C.), the founder of Buddhism, achieved enlightenment while sitting under a bodhi tree and thus it has special significance and is held sacred by Buddhists. Page 133.

trek: a journey or trip, especially when difficult or involving hardship. Used figuratively. Page 3.

tremulous: cautious or timid. Page 132.

triggering: causing another event to occur; activating; setting off. Page 117.

tripwire(s): something that activates something else. From the literal meaning of *tripwire,* a wire that is attached to a trap, weapon, alarm, camera or other device in such a way that it will set the device off if disturbed. Page 117.

tumultuous: characterized by tumult (confusion, agitation, disturbance); highly agitated or turbulent. Page 75.

turn (one's) back upon: reject something that one has previously been connected with. Page 125.

turn (something) off: cause to cease operating or appear, as if by means of a switch, button or valve; deactivate. Page 105.

turn on: cause to start operating or appear, as if by means of a switch, button or valve; activate. Page 105.

U

umpteen: a large but unspecified number (of something). Page 22.

unaberrated: not affected by *aberration,* any deviation or departure from rationality. Page 36.

unblemished: not spoiled by wrongdoing or error. Page 142.

underscoring: emphasizing something, likened to marking with a score (line drawn or scratched) underneath the printed words on a page. Page 155.

uneased: not made easier to bear, lightened or lessened. Page 149.

unequivocally: conclusively and absolutely; not subject to conditions or exceptions. Page 9.

unknown: something great and unknown or mysterious; something that is undiscovered or unexplored. Page 21.

un-unified: having specific items of information, data or the like *not unified,* not coordinated, but remaining separate from one another. Page 7.

unwavering: not changing or not being changed; firm and steady. Page 115.

unwitting: unaware of what is happening in a particular situation. Page 81.

unwittingly: unknowingly; unconsciously; without awareness. Page 19.

V

vantage point: a position or location that provides a broad view or perspective of something. Page 124.

vaporings: foolish, empty statements; remarks that have no substance. Page 140.

Veda: the Vedic Hymns, the earliest recorded learned writings. They are the most ancient sacred literature of the Hindus, comprising more than a hundred books still in existence. They tell about evolution, about Man coming into this universe and the curve of life, which is birth, growth, degeneration and decay. The word *veda* means knowledge. Page 18.

Vedics: the people of the Hindu (Indian) culture, their religion and literature, the Veda. *See also* **Veda.** Page 65.

vested interest: a special interest in protecting or promoting that which is to one's own personal advantage. *Vested interests* are those who seek to maintain or control an existing activity, arrangement or condition from which they derive private benefit. Page 130.

Vienna: the capital of Austria, where Sigmund Freud (1856–1939) founded psychoanalysis, emphasizing that unconscious memories of a sexual nature control a person's behavior. Page 75.

villain, dark: a criminal or a person regarded as having evil (dark) tendencies. Page 143.

villainy: evil conduct; extreme wickedness. Page 144.

vista: a mental view covering a wide range of events, experiences, etc. Page 3.

Voltaire: (1694–1778) French author and philosopher who produced a range of literary works, often attacking injustice and intolerance. Page 21.

vortex: a whirling mass (of something) in the form of a visible column or spiral. Page 11.

W

waded through: made one's way slowly as if because of having to push through a large quantity of something. Page 7.

waste, laid to: completely destroyed or devastated (something). Page 77.

waterfront: the part of a town that lies alongside a body of water. Page 47.

wavelength: a wavelength is the distance from the peak (crest) to the peak (crest) of a wave. Wavelength is used here in reference to the specific waves emitted or registered, as on an oscilloscope. *See also* **oscilloscope.** Page 53.

way, pay one's: pay one's own expenses. Page 89.

West Coast: the western coast of the United States, bordering the Pacific Ocean and comprising the coastal areas of California, Oregon and Washington. Page 33.

Western Electric: *Western Electric Company, Inc.,* an American company, major producer of telephone equipment, electronic devices, communications satellites, radar systems and defense equipment such as used in missile systems, nuclear weapons, etc. Page 100.

wheedled: persuaded someone to do something, as with pleasant words; coaxed. Page 83.

whence: from what source, origin or cause. Page 108.

white coats, chaps in: a reference to psychiatrists and their attendants, etc., who characteristically wear white coats. Page 106.

White, William Alanson: (1870–1937) American psychiatrist who, in the early 1900s, was superintendent of St. Elizabeths Hospital in Washington, DC, and professor of psychiatry at the medical schools of Georgetown University and George Washington University. Page 76.

whole track: the individual's entire time track. The *time track* is a record of his consecutive moments of living stretching back as long as he has lived. Page 108.

wide-eyed: having the eyes wide open, as in amazement or wonder. Page 139.

willed: intended or desired (something) to happen; attempted to cause or bring about by an act of the will. Page 11.

Winter, Joseph: a doctor who was involved in and altered Dianetics in the early 1950s. Page 100.

withered: shriveled or shrunken. Page 52.

wit, to: used to introduce a list or explanation of what one has just mentioned. Originally a phrase used in law, *that is to wit,* which meant that is to know, that is to say. Page 33.

would-be: wishing or pretending to be; posing as. Page 140.

woven: introduced or connected into a larger whole. Page 33.

X

X factor: a relevant but unknown element or circumstance. Page 10.

Y

yearnings: deep longings or persistent desires for (something). Page 99.

yeast: a microscopic single-celled organism capable of converting sugar into alcohol and carbon dioxide and hence used for producing alcohol in beer and wine, and for making bread rise. Page 41.

yield(ed): produce or give forth (results, products, etc.). Page 35.

Yogi: someone who practices *yoga*. *See also* **Yogism.** Page 79.

Yogism: the teachings or practice of *yoga,* a school of thought in the Hindu religion and the system of mental and physical exercise developed by that school. Hinduism is the major religion of India and emphasizes freedom from the material world through purification of desires and elimination of personal identity. Hindu beliefs include reincarnation. Page 18.

Z

zygote: a female reproductive cell that has been fertilized by a male reproductive cell. Page 42.

INDEX

A

aberration, 39
    inorganic, 35
    source of, 37

ability
    computational, 41
    Grade IV Release, 122
    state of existence and, 122

Acropolis
    photographs by L. Ron Hubbard, 124, 126–127, 128
    Porch of Maidens, 132

agreement
    human soul and, 79

Alamo, 106

Alexandria
    riots of, 130

American Fiction Guild
    president of, 89

American Medical Association (AMA)
    Dianetics and, 137

American Psychiatric Association (APA)
    Dianetics and, 137

ammonia
    sea of, 129

amnesia, 105

analytical mind
    cells and, 42
    definition, 40
    Dianetics and, 41

Anaximander
    theory of evolution, 22

Ancient Greece
    philosophy and, 125

animal kingdom
    Man and, 42

animals
    state of animal, Man and, 119

answers
    Scientology, 129–131
        attested by results, 130

Arabian Nights, 13

Aristarchus, 20

Aristotle, 20, 125

artificial towers
    of learning, 139

artist
    higher beings and, 120

Asia, 89, 129, 132, 139, 149
    2,500 years ago, 134

Astounding Science Fiction, 18, 33
    John W. Campbell, Jr., and, 100

astronomy, 19

Athens
    seen from the Acropolis, 128

atom bomb, 62

atom disintegrator, 24

attitude
    toward you and toward another, 62

auditing
    definition, 2
    higher state of being and, 120

Auditing Demonstration Room, photograph, 151

auditor, 40

autobiography, 137

awareness
    center of, 40
    10 percent of potential, 39

B

basic intention
    of LRH, 142

Basic Principle of Existence, 88

Bay Head, New Jersey
    photographs of LRH's home, birthplace of Dianetics, 32, 44–47

beauty
    gracing things with magic and, 61

Beethoven
    past lives and, 106

Berkeley, George, 18

birth, 42

"Birth of Dianetics, The," 31–33

Blackfeet
    friendship with, 75

Bodhi, 133

body
    energy mechanism, 63

botany, 24

Bowie, Jim
    past lives and, 106

Bremerton, Washington, 10

bridge, *see* **Scientology Bridge**

Browning, 81

Brown, Professor, 81

Buddha, 120
    Bodhi and, 133

Buddhism, 87

Buddhists, 65
    meditation, 90

C

Camelback Mountain
    photograph of L. Ron Hubbard at, 52–53
    Ron's home, photographs, 60–61, 68–71

Campbell, Jr., John W.
    Astounding Science Fiction editor, 18, 100

case histories, past lives
    Have You Lived Before This Life?, 102
    young girl worried about her "husband and children," 105

Catherine the Great
    past lives and, 106

cells, 42

cereal box
    picture of the picture on, 83

Chaldeans
    astronomy and ancient, 19

cheela, 18

children
- Dynamic Two, 36
- past lives and, 106
- pleasure in life and, 60

Christ
- efforts of, 65

Christians, 65

Christophe, Citadel of a, 80

Church of Scientology
- East Roosevelt Street, 53
- Monroe School, 53
- religious organization of many creeds and faiths, 67

Citadel of a Christophe, 80

civil populations
- slaughter of, 130

Classification, Gradation and Awareness Chart
- photograph of LRH unveiling first, 121

Clear, 36, 41
- definition, 35
- description, 37
- dynamics and, 36
- state of, 122, 133
- to Operating Thetan, 134

collegiate world, 139

communication
- Grade 0 Release, 120
- Man and, 120

Communications Course
- six-year-old boy and, 144

communism
- religions and, 79

conditions
- fixed, moving out of, 122

Cone, Dr. Elbert E.
- dental office, 10

Congressional Airport, 82

Constantinople, Second Synod of, 101

Copernican system, 23

Copernicus, 20
- gravity and, 20

corvette
- Second World War, 89, 146

Cross, Scientology, 3

crystalline spheres, 20
- Ptolemy's theory of, 23

Curtain, the
- land of shades, 11

cycle of birth and death
- freedom from, 133

cytological experiments, 9

D

"Dangerous Dimension, The"
- philosophic fiction, 18

Dark Ages
- superstition of, 125

Darwin, 89

Darwinian theory
- learned responses, 9

dead mathematics
- modern uses for, 139

death
- demystification of, 99–102

defense
- for having lived, 137–145

definitions
- analytical mind, 40
- auditing, 2

Clear, 35
Dianetics, 35
engram, 42
"I," 40
Operating Thetan, 122, 133
philosophy, 1
Release, 35
science, 80
Scientologist, 67
Scientology, 65, 80, 132, 147
scio, 80
spirit, 122, 133
thetan, 122, 133
time track, 40, 122

deluge myth, 31

Democritus, 125
theory of planetary evolution and, 22

"Demystification of Death, The," 99–102

depression
basic causes of, 148

Dharma
efforts of, 65

Dhyana
study of Wisdom, 65

dialectic materialism
religions and, 79

Dianetics
birth of, 31–33
definition, 35
discussion of development of Dianetics and Scientology, 87–91
Individual Dianetics, 35
insignia, 35
materials of, 51
Scientology and beyond, 133–134
symbol, 2, 35
synopsis of, 35–42
techniques, first formal application of, 33
where the subject started, 87

***Dianetics: The Modern Science of Mental Health*,** 90, 137, 148
Bay Head, New Jersey, birthplace of, photographs, 32, 44–47
"Excalibur" and, 10
first edition, 43
national movement, 100
opening synopsis of, 33

Dianetics: The Original Thesis
"Excalibur" and, 10

Durant, Will, 147

dying
process of, 11

Dynamic Four, 36

Dynamic One, 36

Dynamic Principle of Existence, 36, 141
Survive, 89

dynamic(s)
description, 36
Dianetics and, 37

Dynamic Three, 36

Dynamic Two, 36

E

1870
psychologists and, 119

electronics, 125

elephants
seven, on seven pillars, 129

Elizabeth, New Jersey
first Dianetic Research Foundation, 100
photograph of L. Ron Hubbard, 30

Empedocles
    natural selection and, 22

endocrine system
    mental block and, 33
    study of, 90

energy
    Scientology and increased knowledge in, 63

engram
    bank, 39
    definition, 42
    psychosomatic illness and, 105
    therapy and, 40

engramic commands, 41

environment
    building one's own, 61

Eratosthenes, 20

Euclid, 125

exact science
    astronomy, 19

"Excalibur," 13–14
    hilltop writer's retreat, photographs, 6, 16–17
    prefatory note, 11
    Survive and, 7–10

existence
    Dynamic Principle of, 36
    state of, 119

expedition
    Northwest Coast Indian lands, 31

Explorers Club
    LRH anecdotes, 139–140

exterior
    L. Ron Hubbard, first to identify capabilities of exterior beings, 53
    states of existence and, 123

F

failure
    in life, examples, 62

faiths
    Scientology and, 67

"famous person" fixation
    past lives and, 106

fetus
    memory and, 41

First Book
    first Foundation and, 137

Fitzroy Street, London, England
    "Commonwealth Centre" of Scientology, photographs, 110–111

flowers
    remember when you were maybe five years old, 59

Foundation(s)
    early, 90
    First Book and, 137

Founding Church of Washington, DC
    photographs, 76–77, 86, 92–95

freedom
    from upsets of the past, 122
    Grade III Release, 122
    knowledge and, 148
    spiritual, 133
    truth shall set you free, 148
    ultimate truth and, 130
    way to, 149

Freudian theory
    ethnology and, 75

F Street
    salt mines of, 82

function monitors structure, 33

future
  ability to face, 122

G

Gamow, Dr. George
  experiments and atomic bomb, 81
Gautama Siddhartha, 120
  efforts of, 65
George Washington University
  psychology laboratory, 88
  rediscovery of human soul and, 81
Gnostic scriptures
  rebirth of human soul and, 101
goals
  happiness and, 59
  knowing oneself and, 63
Golden Dawn of Scientology, 51–53
"Gott Mit Uns," 129
Grade 0 Release, 120
Grade I Release, 120
Grade II Release, 120
Grade III Release, 122
Grade IV Release, 122
Grade V Release, 122
Grade VA, 123
Grade VI Release, 122
Grade VII, 122
Grade VIII, 123
Greek Philosophy
  goals of, 125
group
  Dynamic Three, 36
group, special-interest, 143

H

happiness
  "Is It Possible to Be Happy?," 59–63
  lies in you, 59
  main problem in life, 59
  making one's life and, 61
  Man and, 148
Harding, Arthur M.
  Astronomy, 20
harmony
  Scientologists live in, 130
Harvey, William, 37, 41
***Have You Lived Before This Life?*,** 102
  first edition, photograph, 103
health
  Scientology's goals exceeding physical, 56
Hebrews
  astronomy and ancient, 19
help
  using wisdom for, 149
Heraclitus, 125
Hermitage House, 90
higher being
  communication and, 120
hilltop writer's retreat
  photographs, 6, 16–17
Himalayas
  savants and, 120
Hindu
  astronomy and ancient, 19
Homer, 20
Homo sapiens
  states of existence higher than, 120

hope
    wisdom and, 149

Hubbard Association of Scientologists
    first organization, Phoenix, Arizona, 91

Hubbard Communications Office of London
    photograph, 101

humanities, 35

human memory
    repository of, 76

I

"I"
    definition, 40

Ice Age
    deluge myth and last, 31

immortality, 131, 133
    L. Ron Hubbard, first to verify, 53
    recognition of, 132

income tax
    world of, 130

Individual Dianetics, 35

inflation
    world of, 130

intelligence
    increases in, 130

intention
    basic intention of LRH, 142

internal-combustion engines
    subject of, 24

internment camps
    prisoners of, 31

Ionian Greeks
    physics and, 22

"Is It Possible to Be Happy?," 59–63
    introduction, 52

-isms, 79

Is there a Hereafter?, 129

ivory tower
    of philosophy, 89

J

Janssen piano, 68

Java
    combat on the island of, 146

John Doe
    can become a higher being, 120

Journal of Scientology
    article, 52

journey
    Ron's philosophic, 2

Judah, Dr. Stillson
    L. Ron Hubbard discusses Dianetics and Scientology with, 87–91
    never previously published conversation with, 3, 87–91
    photograph, 87
    theologian, 3

K

Kant, 88
    psychology and, 22

knowingness
    Scientology and, 65

knowledge
    cumulation of, 23
    of energy, Scientology and, 63
    philosophy and pursuit of, 147

route to freedom and, 148
simple truths, 24
subject of the soul and, 80
unified and un-unified, 21
workability of, 147

Kodiak bear, 140

Koenig photometer, 88
illustration, 81
voice vibrations and poetry, 81

L

Lama priest, 90

lamaseries, Tibetan, 75

land of shades
the Curtain and, 11

language, 39

Lao-tzu
efforts of, 65

lay practitioners
Scientology and, 67

Library of Congress
psychology books and, 88

life
attitude toward, 60
child and putting grace upon, 60
failure in, description, 62
happiness and main problem, 59
making, or being made by, 62
motivating principles of, 89
seeing from top down and the bottom up, 149
Survive and, 14
tests of a life well lived, 137

literati
Dianetics and American, 33

London, England
photograph of L. Ron Hubbard, 98

Los Angeles Daily News
photographs of L. Ron Hubbard, 38–39

Love Thy Neighbor
world today and, 130

L. Ron Hubbard Office
photograph, 150

M

magic, 62
children and, 60
gracing things with beauty and, 61

Man
animal kingdom and, 42
animal, state of, 119
basically good, 41, 133
first state above, 120
matter, state of, 119
mental image pictures and, 90
obsessed with materiality, 149
past upsets, 122
seeking to make into a higher being, 119
states of, 119
understanding the spirit of, 125

Manchuria, 75

Mankind
basic nature, 37
Dynamic Four, 36

"Man's Search for His Soul," 52, 55–57

marriage
not marrying the first one who seemed desirable, 62

not working out, 60

materialist creed

platitudes and, 2

materiality

Man obsessed with, 149

matter

state of, 119

medicine man

"Old Tom," 75

memory

protein molecules and, 84

repository of, 76

restoration of, 105

mental block

endocrine system and, 33

mental image pictures

Man and, 90

"more real" than present time, 105

mind

analytical, 40, 41

conscious, 37

energy in one's, 63

not an unsolved problem, 62

reactive, 37

unconscious, 37

miracles

Scientology and, 52

tomorrow's, 19

Montana

Blackfeet tribesmen in, 75

Moses

efforts of, 65

Moss, Dr. Fred August

George Washington University, psychology department chief, 76, 88

motives

of L. Ron Hubbard, 137

motto

what is, is, 106

mud from there on down, 129

Murphy, Bridey, 105

musician

higher beings and, 120

myelin sheathing, 41

"My Only Defense for Having Lived," 137–145

introduction, 136

"My Philosophy," 147–149

introduction, 146

original handwritten page from, 146

mysticism, 36

mythology

examination of, 31

N

Napoleon

past lives and, 106

Natural Philosophy

science and, 125

Nature, 41

naval hospital

year spent in, 89

Newton

mathematics and, 20

natural laws and, 22

New York City

literary life, 18

Nietzsche, 88

Nirvana, 131

Northwest Coast Indian lands, 31

"Note on Past Lives, A," 105–106

O

Oak Knoll Naval Hospital, 31

"Old Tom"
  folkloric studies with, 75

Old West, 139

-ologies, 79

Operating Thetan (OT)
  cycle of birth and death and, 134
  definition, 122, 133
  mapping route to, 124
  state of, 122

operation, dental, 10
  anesthetic and, 11

optic nerves
  World War II injury to, 149

Organizational Chart, 108

Orient, 83
  study in, 87

oscilloscope
  human spirit and, 53

OT Course, 134

OT Symbol, 3

overrun
  Grades processes and, 123

P

pain, 39

painful emotion, 39

painter
  higher beings and, 120

Parmenides, 125

Pasteur, 41

past lives, 3
  "A Note on Past Lives," 105–106
  board resolution and, 100
  children and, 106
  Christian dogma and, 100
  "famous person" fixation, 106
  Have You Lived Before This Life?, 102
  what they are suppressed by, 105
  young girl worried about her "husband and children," 105

Pelley, 85

philosophy
  capable of being used, 147
  definition, 1, 147
  Greek, 125
  "My Philosophy," 147–149
  of Scientology, 1
  religious, 129
  route to knowledge and, 124
  wins after 2,000 years, 124, 125–127

Phoenicians
  "science fiction" and, 26

Phoenix, Arizona
  Camelback Mountain photographs, 52–53, 60–61, 68–71
  LRH with Scientology students, photograph, 51
  photograph of L. Ron Hubbard, 50

phonograph record
  engram and grooves of, 42

photometer, 81

physical universe
  Man mastering, 63

physics
  Ionian Greeks and, 22
  mathematics and, 87
  terra incognita and, 84

picture of the picture
  on the cereal box, 83

platitudes
    materialistic creed and, 2

Plato, 125
    psychoanalysis written of in *Republic*, 22

pleasure
    child putting grace on life and, 60
    helping others and greatest, 148

poetry
    experiment, 81

polio victims, 102

Polo, Marco, 75

Port Orchard, Washington, 11
    hilltop writer's retreat, photographs, 6, 16–17

Portsmouth
    corvette crew from, 89

positrons
    electrons and, 23

Power
    Grade V Release, 122
    state of, 122

Power Elite, 136

Powerful Unknown, 40

prenatal, 41

Prime Mover Unmoved, 23

problems
    able to make vanish, 120
    Grade I Release, 120
    happiness and main, 59
    Scientology and ability to handle, 130

processing
    goal of, 105

protein molecules
    memory and, 84

psychiatry
    loggerheads to any spiritual movement for individual liberty, 136
    religions and, 79

psychoanalysis, 35

psychologists
    mortal man and, 119

psychology
    religions and, 79

psychosomatic ill(ness), 39, 105
    Clear and, 41
    Dianetics and, 35
    dynamics and, 37
    hidden source, 37
    Release and, 41

psychosurgery
    opposition to, 76

Ptolemy, 20, 23

Puget Sound, Washington
    photograph, 8–9

Pythagoras, 20, 125

R

reactive mind, 116
    cells and, 42
    description, 37
    effect upon the spirit, 133
    eradicating, 133

recordings
    Dianetics and, 42

"Rediscovery of the Human Soul," 79–85
    introduction, 75

reincarnation
    doctrine of, 101
    past lives and, 106

Release, 41
    definition, 35

relief
    able to bring to oneself and others, 120
    Grade II Release, 120

religion
    coming from philosophy, 147
    extinction of, 79
    field of, 90
    interest in field of, 87
    science meeting with, 55
    two categories, 67

religious philosophy, 129

religious sages
    salvation of the human soul and, 65

Republic
    Plato's, 22

research and discovery
    central revelation of, 51

Research Room
    photograph, 151
    Saint Hill Manor, 116

returning, Dianetics and, 40

Rogers, Donald, 100

S

Saint Hill Manor, Sussex, England, 115, 116–117, 150–153
    Auditing Demonstration Room, photograph, 151
    Clears on OT Course, 134
    L. Ron Hubbard Office, photograph, 150
    photographs, 112–113, 115, 116–117, 150–153
    photographs of L. Ron Hubbard, 114, 121, 148
    Research Room, 116
        photograph, 151
    Saint Hill Special Briefing Course, 115

Saint Hill Special Briefing Course, 115

salt mines of F Street, 82

Sanskrit, 65

savants
    amongst the Himalayas, 120

Schopenhauer, 88
    evolution and, 22
    religion and, 20

science
    coming from philosophy, 147
    definition, 80
    of mind, 35
    religion meeting with, 55

scientific truths, 36

Scientologist
    definition, 67
    seldom ill, 130

Scientology
    answers, 129–131
    belief and, 130
    Communications Course, 144
    cross of, 3
    definition, 65, 80, 132, 147
    description, 1
    "Dianetics, Scientology and Beyond," 133–134
    discussion of development of Dianetics and Scientology, 87–91
    Doctor of Divinity, 67
    goals of Greek philosophy and, 127
    Golden Dawn of, 51

increased knowledge of energy and, 63

knowingness and, 65

knowing oneself and, 63

lay practitioners and, 67

materials of, 51

miracles performed, 57

ordained minister, 67

OT Symbol, 3

results from the practice of, 130

route to freedom, 155

states above Man and, 123

symbol, 2

what is new about, 119

where the subject started, 87

why it grows, 131

wisdom and, 67

Scientology Bridge, 117

Classification, Gradation and Awareness Chart, photograph, 121

description, 115

future and, 123

route to awareness and ability, 2

Scientology, 2

scio

definition, 80

Second Synod of Constantinople, 101

self

goal for thousands of years, knowing, 63

sex, 36

Socrates, 125

soul

freed, only effective therapeutic agent, 56

"Man's Search for His Soul," 52, 55–57

"Rediscovery of the Human Soul," 79–85

introduction, 75

scientific subject, 80

studying the, 3, 80

see also **spirit**

South Pacific, 139

special-interest groups, Dianetics and, 143

speculative fiction, 18

Spencer

evolution and, 22

knowledge, unified and un-unified, 21

principles of, 18

Synthetic Philosophy, works of, 7

Spinoza

formulations of, 18

modern psychology and, 22

spirit

behavior of, 91

definition, 122, 133

man and, 91

moral and ethical science and, 91

oscilloscope and, 53

philosophic goal and, 125

reactive mind and, 133

Scientology and, 132

source of all, 51

study of, 3, 80, 88

see also **soul,** 91

spiritual essence

statement on, 51

standard memory banks, 40, 41

states of existence, 119

St. Elizabeths Hospital, 76

stimulus-response

basis, 37

mechanisms, 90

Story of Philosophy, The, 147

sub-mind, 37

superstition, 62

    wisdom and, 149

survival

    common denominator, 89

    entire dynamic urge, 36

    four equations of, 36

Survive and "Excalibur," 7–11

survive and succumb

    motivating principles of life, 89

symbiotes

    dynamics and, 36

symbols

    Dianetics, 2–3, 35

    Scientology, 2–3

synopsis

    of Dianetics, 35–42

T

Tao

    study of Wisdom, 65

Taoism, 87

Taoists, 65

Technical Bulletins

    handwritten, 117

terra incognita

    physics and, 84

tests

    of a life well lived, 137

Thales, 20, 125

therapy

    briefly stated, 40

    description, 40

    goal of, 36

Theta Clear, 55

thetan

    definition, 122, 133

Thetan Exterior

    processes, 123

Thompson

    Commander Joseph Cheesman, 75

    first psychoanalyst of the US Navy, 88

thought, 39

Tibetan lamaseries

    entrance to, 75

time track

    definition, 40, 122

    three conditions concerning, 122

"Tomorrow's Miracles," 19–26

Tower of London, 96–97

truth

    falsehood exposed by, 149

    finding what is true for you, 147

    nature of, 129

    scientific truths, 36

    Scientology and, 56

        attested by results, 130

    sets one free, 130

turtle

    mud from there on down, 129

U

"unconscious" mind, 37

"unconsciousness," 40

understand

    Man liking to, 148

unhappiness

    description, 62

US Navy
    Dr. Thompson, first psychoanalyst of, 88

V

Veda
    study of Wisdom, 65

Vedics, 65

Voltaire, 21

W

war
    uneased by a single word of decency, 149

Washington, DC
    Founding Church, photographs, 76–77, 92–95
    L. Ron Hubbard, photographs in, 74, 86
    Washington Monument, 72

Western society
    the notion of a former existence and, 100

What is Death?, 129

"What Is Scientology?," 65–67
    introduction, 53

Where do I come from?, 129

white coats
    chaps in, 106

White, William Alanson
    superintendent of Washington, DC's St. Elizabeths Hospital, 76

Who am I?, 129

Whole Track Release
    Grade VI, 122

Winter, Dr. Joseph
    first Foundation medical director, 100

wisdom, 65
    hope and, 149
    one line, 13
    philosophy and pursuit of, 147
    Scientology and, 67

womb
    longing for, 42
    memories of the, 41

world
    living in a very fast-paced, 62
    remember when you were maybe five years old, 59

X

X factor, 10

Y

Yogi, 79

Yogism, 18

Z

zygote
    human cells and, 42

THE
L. RON HUBBARD
SERIES

"To really know life," L. Ron Hubbard wrote, "you've got to be part of life. You must get down and look, you must get into the nooks and crannies of existence. You have to rub elbows with all kinds and types of men before you can finally establish what he is."

Through his long and extraordinary journey to the founding of Dianetics and Scientology, Ron did just that. From his adventurous youth in a rough and tumble American West to his far-flung trek across a still mysterious Asia; from his two-decade search for the very essence of life to the triumph of Dianetics and Scientology—such are the stories recounted in the L. Ron Hubbard Biographical Publications.

Drawn from his own archival collection, this is Ron's life as he himself saw it. With each volume of the series focusing upon a separate field of endeavor, here are the compelling facts, figures, anecdotes and photographs from a life like no other.

Indeed, here is the life of a man who lived at least twenty lives in the space of one.

FOR FURTHER INFORMATION VISIT
www.lronhubbard.org

To order copies of *The L. Ron Hubbard Series*
or L. Ron Hubbard's Dianetics and
Scientology books and lectures, contact:

US AND INTERNATIONAL

BRIDGE PUBLICATIONS, INC.
5600 E. Olympic Blvd.
Commerce, California 90022 USA
www.bridgepub.com
Tel: (323) 888-6200
Toll-free: 1-800-722-1733

UNITED KINGDOM AND EUROPE

NEW ERA PUBLICATIONS
INTERNATIONAL ApS
Smedeland 20
2600 Glostrup, Denmark
www.newerapublications.com
Tel: (45) 33 73 66 66
Toll-free: 00-800-808-8-8008